GETTING TO THE PROMISED LAND WITHOUT SPENDING FORTY YEARS IN A WILDERNESS

GETTING TO THE PROMISED LAND WITHOUT SPENDING FORTY YEARS IN A WILDERNESS

by

The Rev. Michael Schulenberg

DORRANCE PUBLISHING CO., INC.
PITTSBURGH, PENNSYLVANIA 15222

For information or to order additional books, please write:
Dorrance Publishing Co., Inc.
701 Smithfield Street
Third Floor
Pittsburgh, Pennsylvania 15222
U.S.A.
1-800-788-7654
Or visit our web site and on-line catalog at www.dorrancebookstore.com

Dedicated with affection for
and gratitude to Karen, my wife,
and our children, David and Melissa

ACKNOWLEDGMENTS

I wish to express my gratitude to the following for their assistance, guidance and fellowship. From such has come this work.

- The parishes of St. Paul's Episcopal Church, Flint, Michigan; St. Mark's Episcopal Church, Aberdeen, South Dakota; Christ Episcopal Church, Red Wing, Minnesota; and Holy Cross Episcopal Church, Pensacola, Florida.
- The Adult Christian Education Foundation, home of *The Bethal Series*, Madison, Wisconsin.
- The Rev. George Schulenberg and the Rev. Wayne Hepler, mentors for my spiritual journey.
- Drs. Jan and Bill Martin who helped organize and order the manuscript.
- Mr. and Mrs. Britt Landrum whose final encouragement made possible the completion of this publication.

And to my wife, Karen, my eternal gratitude for her witness of Love.

CONTENTS

CONTENTS

INTRODUCTION

...an Ethiopian eunuch, a minister and in fact the treasurer to Candace, queen of the Ethiopians, was on his way home after coming to Jerusalem to worship. He was sitting in his carriage reading the prophet Isaiah. The Spirit said to Philip, 'Approach this carriage, and keep close to it.' Then as Philip ran forward he heard the man reading the prophet Isaiah, and he said, 'Do you understand what you are reading?' And he replied, 'How can I unless I have someone to guide me?' – Acts 8:27-31

Reading the scriptures, listening to a sermon, "figuring out" our own faith (let alone *the* faith) is more often than not similar to sitting in an open carriage behind a horse on a hot summer day seeking enlightenment. The ever-present flies of the air seem to swirl in our minds. Truth succumbs to frustration, or worse, to simplicity. The freedom promised to the children of God is buried in confusion as we wander like lost souls in a desert of words and clichés.

How similar is the forty-year trek of the Hebrews in their exodus from Egypt to the journey of far too many Christians in these first years of the twenty-first century. A journey that could have been accomplished in a matter of months took forty long years, a span of time in which those born into slavery in Egypt died without seeing the realization of God's new land, leaving only those born upon the journey and whose memory was to be fashioned solely out of the experiences of their God's all-encompassing providence as the recipients of Moses' great vision. It took a lifetime, forty years, for some to get to the Promised Land.

We, too, are promised a kingdom and an inheritance befitting the sons and daughters of the living God. And it, like the land of Canaan for the Hebrews so long ago, is ours by the promise of God. It cannot be withheld from us. It can, however, be so camouflaged that it never be revealed in the image and vision proclaimed to us by the word of our God! Such, I believe, is the experience of our day. It is an era of wrestling, more so of fighting, for the kingdom in the face of countless roadblocks and traps set for weary travelers. It is an age in which the spiritual markers on the roads are written in conflicting claims, where contrasting religious language and new "works and signs" are required of those willing to make the trip, all of which are landmarks as useless and lifeless as the law which failed our spiritual forefathers.

"How shall I find *my* way unless I have someone to guide me?"

The thoughts that follow are shared that you might find today a relationship with your Creator; that you might experience the life of the kingdom of God; and that you might know the purpose of your new birth in Christ and the Love of God for you in this life as well as in the eternity that follows.

CHAPTER ONE
CREATED IN HIS IMAGE

When a child is born, one often hears, "Why he looks just like his father!" Or, it could be like the mother, or the grandmother, or whoever. Thankfully, my children look like their mother. The point is, we human animals carry on the genetic patterns of our predecessors, not only in looks but also in the less obvious qualities of behavior and attitude. As the mysteries of genetic coding are being solved, our inherited histories from generations uncounted reveal for each of us the propensities for physical, mental, even emotional replication of life. We *are* the accumulated result of countless generations of parents.

It is known that children of families with a history of alcoholism are more prone to have problems with alcohol than children without such a history. The same is true for children of families where heart disease or certain kinds of cancer have occurred. We inherit from the generations that precede us the things that affect us and the generations yet to come. Fabres disease affects only males but is passed through females; mothers pass it on to their sons in the families where it exists. Sickle-cell anemia is found only amongst people of black-African heritage. There are countless other examples but the point, I think, is made. We do carry on the image of those who have gone before us.

Our Hebrew forefathers may have pondered this in a more particular fashion, I suspect, when viewing the civility of life in their midst, wondering why the emotions involved with living one with another never seemed to grow healthier. The conflicts in family relationships are the stuff of the earliest stories of Genesis and continue throughout the whole of sacred writ. Adam accuses Eve; Cain kills Abel; Jacob cheats his brother, Esau. One would think that growing up with such pain and sorrow would be enough to cause someone to cry out, "No more! I'll not live like my parents have lived! I'll be different!" Yet, when the pain eases and the tears are dried, more times than not, the son is just like the father, the daughter like the mother, or even worse. Hence, the Hebrew concludes, that God

— *"visits the iniquity of the fathers upon the children and the children's children, to the third and fourth generation."*[1]

1

In our generation, we are only beginning to recognize the complexity and magnitude of the problems of child and spouse abuse and coming to an understanding that most abusive people were themselves the victims of abuse, too often by members of their immediate family. Thus, it is true to say that like it or not, we do physically and emotionally bear the images of our parents and grandparents and more.

Understanding the reality of imaging, therefore, is crucial for coming to grips with our own personal identity and for dealing with the choices each of us make consciously or unconsciously between good and evil, right and wrong—the spiritual stuff of our life journeys. "Who I am," the spiritual question, is specifically answered in the scriptures and done so in a way as to empower each of us to cherish a self-identity that can withstand every affront of a cruel and deceptive world.

A. Genesis 1:26 says,
— *"Then God said, 'Let us make man in our image, after our likeness;.... So God created man in his own image, in the image of God he created him; male and female he created them.'"*

The foundational statement of humanity is that we are created in the image of God. One of the ways that Webster's defines image is, "the optical counterpart of an object, produced by a lens, mirror, or other optical system." Thus stated, we are the mirror reflection of the reality of God. This is not to say that we look like God in some physical sense, however. God is not male or female, human, or flesh and blood. No, our looking like God, our being created in his image, constitutes a completely different dynamic. We are talking of a reality that renders all arguments of creation versus evolution utterly senseless, an exercise in absurdity that our Hebrew forebears could not have dreamed of, for the revelation of creation that they so eloquently portrayed in the stories of our beginnings was (and is) a revelation of God and His nature and not a portrayal of man and his history.

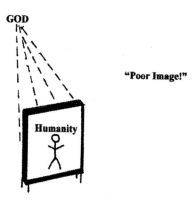

"Poor Image!"

In writing that humanity is created to reflect the reality of God, the author of scriptural truth says we reflect, or mirror, his image. Looking closely, we see that this image is a plural image: "Let us make man in *our* image," and "in the image of God he created *him*; male and female he created *them*." God is an "us" and the image of the creative word is a "them." How interesting. The image of God is a relational image, something that takes two or more to reflect. It has nothing to do simply with my creation but rather with what I create in relationships in and with the world around me. It was neither Adam nor Eve who were important or the purpose of God's creativity but rather the relationship that existed between them. I believe that relationships, the quality and the holiness of them, were what God intended to be His image, for only a relationship could perfectly mirror back to God what was existent in the "us" of the Godhead.

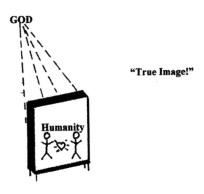

"True Image!"

Said differently, it is this:
— "*At the beginning, God expressed himself. That personal expression, that word, was with God, and was God, and he existed with God from the beginning. All creation took place through him, and none took place without him. In him appeared life and this life was the light of mankind.*"[2]

This familiar passage from the prologue of the Gospel of John reveals to the Christian family that the Son of Man who is born in our midst is the Son of God who is eternal in the Godhead. God as Father and God as Son are one and eternal and they together are existent before the creation of all that is created. I'm reminded of the looks of utter confusion that always grace the faces of thirteen-year old confirmands as they look for the first time at the Athanasian Creed. "Say what? Run that by me again!" The Son of God existed in the mystery of Trinity as Father-Son-Spirit "in the beginning." Father and Son are the "us" of that creation story of Genesis who exist in the relationship of absolute unity and love (remember that John speaks of God in this way in his first pastoral letter, 4:16) and it is precisely that, the relationship of absolute love, that is the image which God seeks to see in His creation.

3

As we follow the creation story in the book of Genesis, we see that it was as God intended. Adam and Eve are perfectly innocent with and to each other; they are unashamed in the presence of their Creator and in the presence of one another; they have nothing that needs to be hidden from the sight of Creator or creation. How wonderful it is when love can stand nakedly innocent and perfect unity exists! Maybe it is like watching a young child who innocently runs naked through the meeting of the Thursday Noon Ladies Literary Club on the way to the kitchen for a cookie. What is the fuss? How can we look aghast at a two year old who is hiding nothing, more so, who has nothing in need of hiding? God's love, perfect love, casts out all fear and shame. There is no need for guilt for there exists no break in the relationships of the beloveds.

This is what the New Testament also says to us. Jesus, whom St. Paul calls the second Adam, comes to reveal God to us. He is born to show the full image of God in the fullness of his own flesh. Here, too, the likeness is not in the attributes of physical looks, but rather in the quality of personality, the soul, the individual self that exists in the flesh as one acts out life in love, kindness, gentleness, forgiveness, etc. (see the list of life that St. Paul speaks of in Galatians 5:22-23). If envy might be termed an acceptable quality once in a while, then I envy the author of the Gospel of John who reveals himself as "*the disciple whom Jesus loved*,"[3] and who experienced the sublime joy of "*lying close to the breast of Jesus*."[4] No wonder he (or a disciple of his) could write that "*God is love*."[5] He experienced it; he knew it in the depth of his soul because he lived it in a relationship with the man, Jesus. Jesus revealed God, his Father, through the relationship of love. The image of creation is fulfilled just as it was intended to be "in the beginning." The God whom we are called to love with all our heart and to worship with all our life is seen in Jesus as he lives out his life; to see one (Jesus) is to see the other (the Creator-God).

And then, this Son of God says something to his disciples that makes it even clearer.

— "*Where two or three are gathered in my name, there I am in the midst of you.*"[6]

We are not ever given grace to think that somehow each of us personally reveals God. No, the reflection of the living God is revealed in and through us where loving relationships exist, where the very Spirit of the God of creation breathes love and life into the daily walk of a man or woman with their brothers and sisters, where two or more people seeking to honor their creator are committed to experiencing kindness, hope, and love together, neither withholding from the other anything that is needed for life nor hiding anything that would injure or destroy the other. A nakedness of soul exists in the Creator's name that creates in the midst of the people the visible expression of God's kingdom of love that God Himself can embrace and then declare, "It is good."

B. There is another powerful way of coming to grips with our own personal identity that is revealed in the scriptures. It begins with the person of Moses and his confrontation with God at the burning bush on Horeb, the mountain of God. God brought Moses to Himself and asked of him the responsibility of rescuing the Hebrew people enslaved under pharaoh in Egypt. Moses was caught in the same self-effacing posture that afflicts so many of us:

— *"Who am I that I should go to pharaoh and bring the sons of Israel out of Egypt?"*[7]

When we have forgotten or never learned that we are created with the grace to reveal the living God, our self-worth registers a negative sound. Worse yet, when we exist in such a way that we reflect the image of another father, our self-image takes on a worse-than-negative image, but that is another story (one that will be dealt with in chapter two on death). Anyway, there was Moses searching for a way to get out from under the call of God. Failing in his first attempt, he tried this tack hoping to convince God into seeking someone else to send:

— *"If I come to the people of Israel and say to them, 'The God of our fathers has sent me to you,' and they ask me, 'What is his name?' what shall I say to them?" God said to Moses, "I AM WHO I AM." And he said, "Say this to the people of Israel, 'I AM has sent me to you.'"*[8]

Here was something totally new for the people of God. The God of Abraham, Isaac, and Jacob had revealed Himself in such a way that would become a part of Israel's deepest identity. God is the great **I AM** of the chosen ones. The unspeakable name of God that we now refer to as Yahweh is somehow wrapped up in this revelation to Moses for the sake of Israel, and centuries later it would still carry with it a power to move God's people, both for good and for ill.

I AM WHO I AM. God. The One who creates and the One who recreates. Scripture and faith lay countless names to God that describe the qualities of His being, all with the ability to show us some facet of His nature. Yet here is a name that essentially carries not a description but rather the very heart of God. **I AM WHO I AM.** Nothing more, nothing less. God. This name, revealed directly to Moses, would become absolutely etched in the mind of Israel with such force that even to speak it would be blasphemous, let alone to somehow identify with it.

Yet, if we, the created crown of God's endeavors, are to reflect His image, must we not be able to reflect His very nature in our hearts as well? If the One whom we are to reflect says, **"I AM WHO I AM,"** why do we say, "I am a nobody?" Why do the souls of countless saints wallow in self-pity and low self-esteem? And why do we as Christian people see as one of Christianity's chief tenents that we are sinners first, last, and foremost?

In the fullness of time came one born of the Spirit of God. Jesus, son of Mary the virgin betrothed to Joseph of the house of David, was born with God, the great **I AM**, as his father. Very powerfully, his life unfolded with the same direction given to all humanity—that of revealing one's father. But for the first time, the nature of the father that was being revealed was different. He who always was, the One who is above all creation, who alone reveals no one but Himself, was now being revealed in His only begotten son, the firstborn of all creation. The image given to Adam was born in Jesus and it was his very nature to reveal it. How wonderful sounding are the words the child Jesus said to his mother,

— *"Did you not know that I must be in my father's house?"*[9]

Mary might very easily have thought as so many mothers do, "He's the spitting image of his dad!"

The man Jesus was more direct than the boy. We soon hear him say things that have to do with identity more than time, place, or activity.

"He who sees me sees the Father[10] *... I and the Father are one*[11] *... that they may be one even as we are one."*[12]

It was with such remarks that Jesus identified himself to the world. He very confidently said in effect, "I know who I am."

It sounds easy, so very easy, this work of self-identification. Yet most of us struggle terribly at it, finding a positive self-image only in relation to some exterior criteria of skill or talent and then only when accompanied by someone else's evaluation of such criteria's worth. The crux of the matter is that our foundational self-image, or our identity, is not something that is given us from without but rather is something that is born from within. The question of Pilate to Jesus at his trial was a real one, for Pilate had no externals regarding Jesus at that moment with which to identify him. *"Who are you?"*[13] Jesus had no need to answer. He knew who he was, then and eternally.

The Gospel of John helps us to see this theme of identity more clearly. How have the people come to know him? He was a teacher, a healer, a friend, and a brother. The people were beginning to think that he was a prophet, indeed maybe one of the great prophets come back from the dead. Jesus had already used such terms as "Son of man" to describe himself and along the way Peter would recognize him as the Christ, the Son of the living God. But as John recalls for us, Jesus began to use another way of telling the world who he was. Listen:

— *"I am the bread of life... I am the light of the world... Truly, truly, I say to you, before Abraham was, I am... I am the door of the sheep... I am the good shepherd... I am the resurrection and the life... I am the way, the truth, and the life... I am the true vine, and my father is the vine-dresser."*[14]

I AM! I AM WHO I AM! With increasing power, Jesus told the people who he was, and with ever-clearer vision they began to hear. Some heard and rejoiced that he had come; others called his words blasphemy and sought his death. Few could miss it as his hour drew nearer.

I often hear people say, "I just don't know what it is that God wants me to do?" My response is that they are asking the wrong question. God does not have much concern for what we do or where we do it; His concern centers on who we are. Said another way, it is not a "what" or a "where" or even a "when" but rather a "who." When the issue of who we are is resolved deep within the soul, the issues of what and where fade away.

The Son of God was content to go anywhere and be with anyone because he was always secure in who he was. He ate with the rich and famous. He hung around with sinners. He was unafraid to mingle with the unclean and demon-filled, touching the lepers and loosening the chains of the demented. His itinerary was not according to any thought of wondering where his Creator wanted him, but was instead an itinerary of living, recognizing that Love's image was needed everywhere and anywhere and that all places and people brought opportunity for the healing love of God to be made manifest. Hence, he simply used each day to be himself, wherever he was and with whomever he met. So it is to be with us.

I AM WHO I AM! Jesus was I AM WHO I AM. He was God in the flesh, a man who perfectly reflected through his flesh the image of God in obedient and sacrificial love. He was at last the fulfillment of the creative purpose of God for all humanity, hence the firstborn of all creation, the elder brother of many who were to come.

C. What might our response be to St. Paul's statement that said,
— "It is no longer I that live but Christ who lives in me."[15]

Was Paul doing some theological sleight-of-hand to prove a premise? I think not. I think that Paul had finally found his true self and was rejoicing in it. What he found is the secret hidden for ages in God and now made known and manifest in the life of the Church. It was this revelation of Paul's that we now look at to complete our thinking and our knowledge concerning our true selves being in the image of God.

It is true to say that what each of us thinks about ourselves will affect how we act out our lives. The inner life affects the outer life. How tragic it is when thoughtless parents corrupt the self-image of their child by years of ridicule and negative comments.

— "You'll never amount to anything!... Why are you so stupid? Can't you ever do anything right?... Why can't you be like your sister? You never see her do such dumb things!"

Having been told over and over that you are stupid, careless, no-good, whatever, the inner person who longs to live out life in the flesh takes on the image of what has been so repeatedly mirrored in words. Self-esteem and confidence are beaten away and an image of endless worthlessness is created; what God intended is lost in the lies of our accuser(s). Such a scenario is played out endlessly in the homes of each generation and then reinforced by the added cruelty of a world tainted by prejudice and selfishness. "Who am I?" is a very real cry from the souls of multitudes who long to walk free and offer to their

7

day the wonderful, creative imaginations that originally welled up within them. We will never know what genius and creativity has been lost forever simply because self-worth was crushed through daily, systematic abuse of souls.

The scriptures are silent concerning the childhood of Jesus and the home in which he grew up. But by the testimony of the Gospels concerning Jesus the man, one can envision that the words of the angels to Mary concerning the child of her womb were something told and retold within the family as Jesus grew. Surely, Mary would have related to Jesus how special a child he was, how that his father was not Joseph but through the miracle of the Spirit's visitation was the God of their people, Yahweh, the great **I AM**. How often might he have heard that his life held specific meaning because of who he was and that the prophets had said specific things concerning his life and work. I think it is safe to say that Jesus was never called "stupid, dumb kid" by Mary or Joseph nor told "you'll never amount to anything."

— *"And Jesus increased in wisdom and in stature, and in favor with God and man."*[16]

The scriptures tell us that a man named Saul was confronted by an unusual experience on a road to Damascus while en route to arrest followers of the Way for persecution by the Jewish hierarchy. Struck blind and knocked to the ground by the event, Saul learned that it was Jesus who confronted him and that he was being chosen in this experience for a special work of God. Taken from there to Damascus, where he was to meet a disciple of Jesus named Ananias, Saul began the transformation in soul that led to the Paul we know in the scriptures. Under Ananias, he began to reread the prophets and reexamine the law; he heard the stories of Jesus and learned what he taught concerning Israel and Israel's God; and ultimately Paul learned first-hand from the risen Christ (through the mystery of the Spirit) the life that the children of God are called to live out and the calling that shall rest on them as the new Israel. Strengthened with such, he began to teach and preach the life he once persecuted.

Stripping aside much of the facade of Paul, we find his teaching to be a continuation of what Jesus said. Recalling that Jesus told Nicodemus that he must be born anew of water and the Spirit, hear what Paul said:

— *"Now we have received the Spirit which is from God, that we might understand the gifts bestowed on us by God... we have the mind of Christ... Do you not know that you are God's temple and that God's Spirit dwells in you?... God's temple is holy and that temple you are... If anyone is in Christ, he is a new creation... we are ambassadors for Christ, God making his appeal through us... All who are led by the Spirit of God are the children of God... you have received the spirit of sonship... it is the Spirit himself bearing witness with our spirit that we are the children of God, and if children, then heirs, heirs of God and fellow heirs with Christ."*[17]

It is no wonder that Paul should say that he was no longer the Saul that had previously existed, but that he was God's son and child, "Christ in me."

Herein is the mystery *"hidden for ages and generations but now made manifest,"* the wondrous good news of our faith: *"Christ in you [us], the hope of glory"*.[18]

What Paul experienced and believed and then lived out was that his very being, his soul, was reborn into that which was of God, just as was true of Jesus who was born of God in the flesh. "God is my father." is something I believe that Paul could say; "I am born of him and am his son." Something of the reality of this kind of theology opened the eyes of Paul to know and to see this mystery, forsaken and forgotten from the beginning when humanity lost the nature to be the image of God and took on the image of a lie and of the impostor. What was lost "back then" was never again seen until Jesus came and, like a little leaven, began the process afresh of making God's likeness known on earth as it is in heaven. His prayer, that the *"glory thou hast given me, I have given to them,"*[19] was true and was happening in the Church; Paul was living proof of it.

Paul and the whole New Covenant community witnessed to the reality of humanity's second birth in Christ. The old life was put to death, sharing the death of Jesus at the cross, and a new life begun through the power of God's indwelling Spirit, present in the resurrection. The *"promise of the Father"*[20] was for all humanity and that first community of believers, knowing Jesus and therefore what God's image looked like, gave visible testimony to the presence of God as they reflected love to their world after Pentecost through acts of charity, righteousness, and mutual self-giving. Paul would write to the Church in Corinth that we do not simply act righteously but rather that *"we have **become** the righteousness of God."*[21]

What all this means, this testimony of Paul and the testimony of countless saints down through the centuries, is that God has made possible a new identity for us that can change our lives by changing the self-image that we have of ourselves. Irrespective of the circumstances of our past, regardless of the conditions of the world into which we have been born, no matter what the conditioning that we have received at the hands of thoughtless and selfish people, we can reflect the very nature of God. By the Creator's Spirit that dwells within us we can become the new creation Christ's passion has procured.

That Spirit allows us to say, "I am all right. I am a child of God. I am His child. I am who I am." I am who I am—**I AM WHO I AM**. God revealed Himself to Moses in this fashion. Jesus revealed himself to the world in this fashion. Paul revealed himself in this fashion in his acknowledging the mystery of "Christ in me" as his new and true identity. You and I can find our true lives in this fashion by confessing the presence of Christ in our lives. "I am the son/daughter of God! I am the beloved child of God! I am presently, eternally, the child of my heavenly Father!" Believing such, I can begin to act as such. So did Paul. So did Jesus. So can you.

Humanity, created in the image of God, failed to be what God had created humanity to be. In the fullness of time, God entered into human flesh to reclaim this portion of His creative purpose. Jesus, God With Us, revealed God in word (as the **I AM** of history) and in deed (reflecting perfectly the loving and righteous relationships existent in the Godhead). Through the death and resurrection of Jesus, the way was made possible for the promise of God—the Holy Spirit—to be poured out on all flesh. Filled with the glory of our Creator, we, the children of God, can experience the freeing grace and knowledge of our true selves, knowing an identity not formed through sin and pain but formed of the loving indwelling of God. The self finds its healing, the image of eternal love is restored, and we can again go about the task of tending a kingdom that is the paradise of God.

CHAPTER TWO
YOU SHALL DIE

I want to take you back now to the story of creation as found in the book of Genesis. Remember, we used it to talk of imaging, being created by God to mirror back to Him His very nature in our relationships with others and the created world we live in. The Hebrew rightly understood this revelation of God and knew in the deepest recess of his soul that this is how things ought to be. Yet looking all around in the real world, it did not take much to drive home the truth that things were far different than God intended. What went wrong? From whence came pain and sorrow; from what evil hand came suffering and sickness; why did man war against his neighbor in an endless cycle of hate?

And humanity's end? When the breath of our being ceases and we go to the grave, what then? Are we like the grass that withers and blows away, never to be known again? Is our existence so fleeting and meaningless that it begins without purpose and ends without remembrance? Is there an answer? There was and there still is an answer consistent with the scriptures. Using the statement of God that one would die when one became disobedient to the relationship of love, this chapter deals with the primal fear of us all, with *death*, and puts the definition of death into a perspective wherein its sting is forever removed and whereby we can understand it and the reality of the grave in a healthy and hopeful way.

Genesis 1 says that man was created in the image of God; male and female God created them. Genesis 2 then tells another creation narrative to talk of the creation of man and the work God planned for him to do. It says that the man, Adam, was placed within a garden or in a place called Eden where, with God, he was to have responsibility and authority to order and care for what God had already accomplished. Further, he was to embellish upon the work God had done by subduing what was not already ordered, taking dominion over plant and animal and every living creature, naming and identifying all things, and then replenishing and reproducing everything, even himself, in accord with God's plan. (We, His created image, were in reality to be co-creators with Him!) To do so, Adam and God were to talk constantly and together hold forth a vision of how paradise should look as a place of beauty and peace.

The Hebrew author understood that man, as a reflection of God, was subordinate to and dependent on God, and that the relationship had meaning and life only in so far as man maintained his obedience to that created relationship. Like an image in a mirror or a shadow attached to its origin, Adam was to his Maker! Life came *to* man in this original endeavor, not *from* man! The author shows it this way:

— *"The Lord God took the man and put him in the garden of Eden to till it and keep it. And the Lord God commanded the man saying, 'You may freely eat of every tree of the garden; but of the tree of the knowledge of good and evil you shall not eat, for in the day that you eat of it you shall die.'"*[22]

It is here that the author of scripture begins to show what went awry with the activity of imaging.

A. Whose image do you and I put forth? We have already stated that we carry on the image of our fathers. Jesus used this thought widely as he identified himself, saying often and in many ways that he reflected his heavenly father, and that if one wanted to see or know God, all one needed to do was to look at him (Jesus). Because of this reflection of God in the flesh of the man, Jesus, other people looked somewhat less in the reflection they portrayed in their own flesh, and the difference became more and more blatant as Jesus' ministry unfolded. So much so, that it caused either of two reactions in the people: for some, it revealed their shortcomings and their failures (called sins), and they asked what they must do to enter the kingdom of God or what works they must do to be doing the will of God. Others, however, found discomfort in the example of Jesus because the light of his life showed the terrible darkness of their own, and they sought to quiet him and discredit his witness. It was to this latter group that Jesus boldly identified the problem; it was one of imaging. In the gospel of John, we find Jesus talking to some of the Jews who had believed in him (John 8:31-59). At verse 38, Jesus said,

— *"I am telling you what I have seen in the presence of my Father, and you are doing what you have seen in the presence of your father.... You are doing your father's work... If God were really your Father, you would have loved me. For I came from God; and I am here. I did not come of my own accord—he sent me and I am here. Why do you not understand my words? It is because you cannot hear what I am really saying. Your father is the devil, and what you are wanting to do is what your father longs to do. He always was a murderer, and has never dealt with the truth, since the truth will have nothing to do with him. Whenever he tells a lie, he speaks in character, for he is a liar and the father of lies."*

Put yourself in the place of those to whom Jesus was speaking some twenty centuries ago. "You are of your father, the devil." I beg your pardon! How does Jesus dare say that I am, or you are, of the devil? That is more of a problem to me than his saying that he is of God, for his statement about us personalizes what might have been a purely academic treatise and something I could take or leave at will. But not now! He said that my father, and yours, is the devil. How can he do that?

Well, really it is quite plain and more than true. He is talking of the image again. Let us go back to the story of creation that our Hebrew forefathers have so eloquently told and examine more closely the truth of its revelation.

God had spoken to Adam about the care of creation in chapters 1 and 2 of Genesis. He had given Adam great freedom to come and go as he wanted and to exercise considerable creativity within the scheme of things. There was just the one injunction limiting Adam's activity, the one concerning the two trees in the garden's center, and in particular relating to the tree of the knowledge of good and evil.

Chapter 3 began with Adam's helpmate, Eve, chatting with a new character in the garden, a serpent of considerable charm. His presence complicated the issue, for just as Adam and Eve enjoyed a relationship with the living God as He met them in the cool of the day and thus grew in reflecting His words, so now do we see a conversation that caused Eve to begin the process of reflecting the words of another.

If ever the truth of incarnation that we have learned in the birth of the Word made flesh, Jesus, should hit home, it must become recognizable here. Adam and Eve could have grown in the incarnation of their relationship with God, the words of His presence taking shape in their flesh as they shared the garden of love and innocence. Instead, the words of a deceiver, a liar, took heart in Eve, and then also in Adam, and in their flesh they began to reflect a deceiver's image. Said another way, they who could have reflected back to God an image of eternal Love and faithfulness allowed another, that serpent the devil, to enter between that relationship and thus cause another reflection to be seen in the flesh of humanity.

Imaging is not a complicated idea. A mirror only reflects back what is put in front of it, neither adding to it nor taking away from it. If I have too many pounds around the midriff, I cannot blame the mirror for showing it nor expect the mirror to hide it. The mirror reveals what is, either good or bad. God created man to mirror, imitate, His nature, and "in the beginning" it was as God intended. But as a mirror can reflect anything that is held up to it, so, too, was it possible for man to mirror another image if the image were interjected in such a way as to come between the relationship first sought.

It is this interjection between God and man that the serpent accomplished in his afternoon dalliance with Eve. She began to reflect, to image, the serpent and his deception and lies and then took the fruit of that image in her flesh to Adam and he ate. Immediately they saw each other different-ly and, not liking the image, they began the process of hiding the truth. First came the clothes, then the hiding from God as He came in the cool of the day. Last, but not least, came the hiding in lies as God asked them about their new appearance.

"It's not my fault," claimed Adam. "The woman you gave to me made me do it!" "Don't blame me," claimed Eve. "The snake made me do it!" What was it that Jesus said? "I know who your father is (or, I recognize the image in you)... for he is a liar and the father of lies."

And so it went. Our beginnings were now wrapped up in a cycle of dis-obedience and lies that caused our spiritual and historical forebears to not only image the liar for a moment but quite literally allowed that image to become their very nature as they guiltily squirmed in the presence of the Love that gave them life. The story suggests that a great moment in our spir-itual beginning was lost because of *this* experience of imaging. In the lies, in the hiding, God saw only the reflection of another who was *"rebellious from the beginning,"*[22] to quote another story (from The Revelation), and He could not bear it or allow it to continue. Hence, the story of creation ends with the expulsion of Adam and Eve from the garden

"lest he (Adam) put forth his hand and take also of the tree of life and live for-ever"[23] in the image of the deceiver. Humanity is separated from a living rela-tionship with the creator.

A simple illustration of that story of expulsion from Eden might help here and make the definition of death something we can understand in a new paradigm.

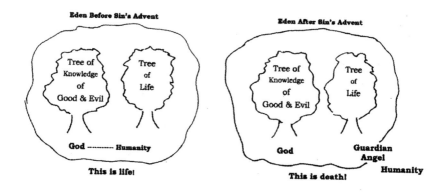

B. *"...in the day that you eat of it you shall die."*

Here is the first biblical reference to death. On the day that Adam was to touch and eat of the fruit of the tree of the knowledge of good and evil he would die. "In the *day*." You know the story that has been told. She ate, he ate, and on the same day they died. "Hold it!," you say. "The story says that on the day they ate they were banished from the garden." True. On the day they ate they were banished from the garden. They died! This is the truth of the story and it is the truth of what God said would happen if they did not reflect His image. Let us look at this in some depth.

Adam and Eve died on the day of their disobedience and refusal to repent. Biblically, death has nothing to do with the terminal moment of existence of the physical body. It relates to our relationship with God, or more accurately, to the absence of our relationship with God. To relate to God face to face is life; to be apart from Him and denied a relationship of walking in innocence with Him in His presence is death. Death is separation from God!

Adam and Eve died as they were expelled from the garden and continued in death all the remainder of their days until, after some nine hundred thirty years and several sons and daughters later, their bodies returned to the dust of the earth from which they were made. Notice that I have purposely tried to choose a specific language to describe Adam's demise. He went to the grave after nine hundred and thirty years; he had been dead since the day of his disobedience.

Death is separation from God!

— "*Sin pays its servants: the wage is death.*"[24]

Adam bought into a package for which God required he pay. He sinned, he was separated, he died.

How different this is from what we normally understand about death. Our contemporary understanding of death has to do with the cessation of our bodily functions and the termination of our physical existence in time. When the heart stops its beating, when the brain ceases its activity, when the lungs no longer fill with air and our body collapses never to rise again, we die. Call the priest and call the funeral director, for death has come. Certainly this thought, too, is scriptural, this understanding of death. The claim that Adam went to the grave after nine hundred and thirty years is stated in Genesis 5:5 as, ". . . *and he died.*" But herein the thought of death reveals what must have been the terror of Adam's day and ours. Where do we go when we pass through the gate of the grave? What becomes of us? The sting of death is not in the giving up of the spirit but rather in the unknown of life without God. I suspect that our man Adam could cope with his separation while in the prime of his health for surely God would have him back, if not today then maybe tomorrow. Youth never pays much mind to death, whatever definition is laid to it. But age does! The passing of days and years causes us to remember more vividly that night after night we are alone and that another cool evening has passed without a word from the Creator. The separation that we have consciously forced into the background of our lives now comes forth again with all its vivid truth: we are alone! If another day does not come, what then? The reality of what death has always been comes home to rest. I am separated: from God, from the human family, from all creation. I am dead.

Though the creation story must remain silent concerning what might have been if Adam and Eve had remained obedient, whether they would have existed in the flesh forever or not, I personally believe that the dust they were created from would have been the dust to which they would have returned in the loving plan of God. Certainly other parts of the created order changed substance in the scheme of things. Seeds and fruits were eaten, plants were used by man and beast alike as food. The creation was to be subdued and used and changed by God's command to Adam, His steward and child. But change of substance and change of order had no fear in that God was present in the change just as He was present in the creation. He was part of what was, one with what is, and would be there in whatever was to be. Hence, if humanity laid down the physical body when it had served its purpose of reflecting the Love and presence of God, such was perfectly all right in that the Spirit breathed into one as he/she became a living being would still be the Spirit that would exist eternally in the loving presence of God.

Certainly it is as easy to conjecture this as it is to say that had Adam not sinned, humanity would have lived in the flesh forever. But scripture states no clear theological conclusion here. And since we biblical people have historically interpreted death only as the cessation of the functions of the body, we have, by our interpretations, unfortunately laid a most malignant story of sin and damnation upon what would later become God's redemptive good news and made the whole notion of death to be something that fails to hold all the true wonder and awe of the New Testament proclamation. Therefore, for the sake of where we are now in this story, let us simply state that all that one can scripturally attest to from Genesis is that regardless of what might have been, death came into the experience of humanity as humanity became disobedient and that the story states only that death was separation from God, nothing more.

When we recognize this sequence of the image of God being replaced in humanity by the image of the father of sin and author of death, and that the death God decreed as the consequence of disobedience was the expulsion from Eden and separation from the intimate fellowship of God our heavenly Father, then it begins to make sense when we talk of original sin or read in the scripture that all have gone astray. After the expulsion from Eden, Adam and Eve set up housekeeping in a strange land and got down to the business of tilling and keeping the land in their own strength. They also got into the begetting business that the Old Testament folk were so good at and brought forth two sons, Cain and Abel. In whose image were they brought forth? As with all of us, in the image of their father, who in this case now reflected the image of the father of lies. Hence, they showed forth what was natural for them and the result was the argument over sacrificial merit that resulted in Cain's murder of Abel. The reflection of what was fallen is now seen in the son as in the father. Sin was in the world and is seen in the flesh from one generation to the next because that is the only image there is on the outside of paradise. St. Paul was correct in saying that,

— *"therefore... sin came into the world through one man and death through sin, and so death spread to all men because all men sinned."*[25]

It is safe to say that Cain passed on the image of disobedience; so did Seth and the other sons and daughters of Adam; so did their children and their children's children, etc.; the shadow comes down even into our own day. We feel born in the image of our fathers in the flesh that still reflects the image of a deceiver rather than the image of our heavenly God. It seems we are separated from God in the same understanding as Adam's separation from God at Eden. We share in the original sin by birth; then often by deed. It is correct to say, even, that we are born into death. Such, anyway, is the legacy of the Old Testament witness and the pre-Christ theology:

— *"Behold, I was brought forth in iniquity, and in sin did my mother conceive me."*[26]

C. The point I wish to hold forth for you, then, is that death in the biblical sense has to do with separation from God and not with the final days of our flesh. To think otherwise changes the whole direction of the revelation of God's gracious acts and confuses the Good News, changing it to a frantic chase of personal immortality rather than a trust in the marvelous love of our God. This shall be dealt with in more detail later. Now, we need to turn to an examination of how God ends the separation and restores His will within His creation.

The history preserved for us in the whole of the Bible is the story of God's plan for reconciling all things to Himself. Beginning with the person of Abram (Abraham), we are told how God created a people for Himself who freely chose to be used by Him for the purpose of restoring life (an innocent relationship with Himself) to the world. In Abraham and his seed forever, God established a covenant, a relationship between two individuals or parties based on solemn promises one to another that bound each to the other for the duration of their lives. This is pretty heady stuff when one realizes that God lives forever. Think about it! The Creator is bound to Israel by a covenant promise not only for the duration of Israel's life but for as long as the Creator exists. What were the promises? *"I will be your God and you will be my people."*[27] With such words came the visions of the restoration of a garden-like paradise in which to live and a loving family with which to share it. The seed of Abraham became the nation, Israel, the progeny of the twelve sons and grandsons of the man, Israel (Jacob), the grandchild of Abraham, and to these people was extended the covenant which God had made. Somehow, in them and through them, God would restore His perfect image and thereby reclaim all creation in His likeness. In so doing, life (reconciliation) would be restored and death (separation) would be ended for all.

However, covenant promises always involve two parties; in this case, God and Israel. Wherein God was faithful to His promises and commitments, Israel failed in hers. Seen through the sacred Law of Sinai, Israel's side of the relationship was a history of failed promises and continued disobedience. Ten simple laws of Love that would reveal God and man in perfect trust and peace were continually broken from the day of their conception. Moses could not even get the law down from the mountain before the people revealed their disregard for the task to which they were called, shattering the spirit of God's will for them even as the tablets of law were shattered in Moses' wrath. It is sometimes hard to admit that old habits are hard to break whereas the law of Love in all its gentle fragility we break with little regard. For Israel, the flesh was weak and continued its bondage to the image of lies and separation.

I leave it to you to review the history of this people as the Old Testament reveals it. It is not only a history of failure regarding the Israelites, but also a history of commitment regarding the covenant of their God. *"I will never remove my steadfast love from Israel,"*[28] says the Lord, and thus through the prophets God began to lay out the future means by which the whole covenant would be upheld and fulfilled. Grace for us all lies in the reality that for the covenant to be fulfilled, Israel's promises had to be fulfilled as well. How this is accomplished is portrayed most clearly in the prophecies of Isaiah wherein the story of the suffering servant is told. Chapters 49-56 describe how God would raise up His servant, Israel, who would fulfill the covenant Abraham made with God and bring life and righteousness to all. By *his* obedience, even in great suffering and rejection, *he* would restore a right relationship with God for all who shall follow (notice the description of Israel changes from plural to singular, from the idea of a nation to that of a person). By *his* suffering we all would be healed. The theology of the New Covenant writers portrays this servant who suffers in our behalf, this Israel of Isaiah, as Jesus.

Let's say this again. No matter how faithful God was to the covenant made with Abraham and his seed forever, the issue would not be settled until both parties fulfilled their promises, and in this matter, the nation Israel was a continual failure. If God was to see the creation restored to a perfect relationship with Himself, He must not only uphold His side of the contract, He must also see that Israel's obligations were upheld as well. To do so required becoming one with Israel, even becoming Israel, so that the covenant of Israel would be fulfilled as promised. God did not do it for Israel; He could not. Israel had to do it herself. But leaving the very nature of deity behind, God entered history in the flesh of one who would not merely represent Israel but would be Israel and live out the covenant promises made by Israel so many generations before. God became the shepherd of His people; He became the servant who suffers; He became the watchman; He became the messiah, Immanuel, who would save His people from their ways.[29]

By now you can see the handwriting on the wall. In the fullness of time was born one who completed the prophetic images and fulfilled the promises of Israel's covenant with the Almighty. It was Jesus. The Son of God was now also the Son of Man. A man in servant's garb fulfilled all that was asked of covenant law. A shepherd of souls laid down his own relationship of safety in eternity to taste the penalty of all creation's disobedience. This is what St. Paul was saying when he wrote,

— *"he... did not cling to his prerogatives as God's equal but stripped himself of all privilege by consenting to be a slave by nature and being born as a mortal man. And, having become a man, he humbled himself by living a life of utter obedience, even to the extent of dying, and the death he died was the death of a common criminal."*[30]

God became man; God left behind Godly powers and was born a human in human flesh with human choices to make. In that human flesh of the man, Jesus, the choices were freely made that fulfilled Israel's ancient covenant with God, and life was restored.

All this is couched for us today in the Christian language of death on a cross and resurrection from the dead. Sadly, this has for centuries carried with it the baggage of damnation to hell or life eternal in heaven, all in the body depending on how one believes. You know what I mean. You're going to die! Where will you go then? Your body will either burn in everlasting damnation or, if you are saved, your body will be raised to a glorious new life in heaven with God. *If* you believe that Jesus died for you, you will be saved. *If* you do not ask him into your life, when you die, you will spend eternity in hell. Simple as that.

No, not simple as that! Jesus' death on the cross is far removed from such simplicity and certainly removed from such judgmental magic. His death on the cross was much more than simply giving up the flesh as his strength ebbed away. Prior to the end of the beating of his heart and the functioning of his mind came an awful moment of *death* which he took upon himself in order to fulfill all scripture: *"Eli, Eli, lama sabachthani?"*[31] Remember this? Where do you hear it? It is read each year on Passion Sunday and again on Good Friday as we follow the story of the betrayal, trial, and crucifixion of Jesus. What does it mean? "My God, my God, why did you forsake me?" Jesus is cast out of paradise (Eden)! Jesus is separated from his Father! Jesus tastes *death*.... for us all. Hear it again! Jesus is forsaken, separated, from God. He dies. Being Israel, he died as the covenant people; all of them.... all of us. In and by his death, he removed the pall[32] that hung over all Israel, old and new, as the just penalty of disobedience; he removed death forever. Separation from God is ended. One man died for/as the nation. It was better that this should happen, so said the high priest at the time.[33] How right he was!

19

When separation was taken for all, Jesus then said, *"It is finished."*[34] What is finished? The problem of what to do with man's disobedience; the holy justice of God which will not allow sin to exist in His presence; the penalty required to prevent disobedient humanity from taking life to itself without first being reconciled in repentance to its creator; the struggle to restore to creation the image of God as intended in the beginning. *"It is finished!"* Now can come, *"Father, into thy hands I commit my spirit!"*[35] And he *"breathed his last."*[36]

Jesus' death on the cross was not his *breathing his last*. Rather, it was his separation from God during those ugly, dreaded minutes. He died in those minutes for all humankind, for you and me. In so doing, he made it possible that separation, *death*, would be no more. God and humanity were one again. You and I were reconciled to the God and father of us all. We will never die. This is how scripture says it:

— *"...because we are convinced that one has died for all; therefore all have died."*[37]

And again,

— *"The death he died, he died to sin, once for all."*[38]

What is more, being raised from the dead, Jesus will never die again. In the death of Jesus was fulfilled that beautiful prophecy of Isaiah 25:6-9. Death (separation) was destroyed on Mt. Calvary, that covering that was cast over all nations. Jesus swallowed up this death forever and wiped away all the tears from our eyes, taking away the reproach of such punishment from all the earth.

Concerning resurrection and life, to these things we will come in later chapters. It must be sufficient only to add here that Jesus was not bound in death but was raised from the dead, heard for his Godly fear, made perfect through his obedience, and the life he lives now he again lives to, in the presence of, God. The event of the resurrection has power and meaning not in terms of immortality but rather in terms of a restored, eternal relationship with God. If death was separation from God, then life has to mean reconciliation back to God. To be alive is to live with, talk to, be one in, and stand innocent before the living God. It cannot be said any better than this:

— *"God was in Christ personally reconciling the world to himself—not counting their sins against them—and has commissioned us with the message of reconciliation... For God caused Christ, who himself knew nothing of sin, actually to be sin for our sakes, so that in Christ we might be made good with the goodness of God."*[39]

D. As in the chapter on imaging, all this is of no real merit unless it experientially applies to us, to you and to me. How sad it would be to have the life of the Christ held before us like a carrot on a stick but be unable to experience it ourselves. If it were just for Jesus, God has played a cruel trick on us. But, thanks be to God, the death he died truly was for us all. It is to this that we now turn.

I want you to know that we, you and I, will never die. Yes, you read this right. We will never die! If that does not sit right with you, try it this way. We have already died and we will never die again. I wish that you would know that for yourself (that is why I am writing this book), for it is the freeing Good News. We will never die! We already did, centuries ago, at Calvary. We all did. Every soul of all creation; all who were, all who are, and all who are yet to come: all died with Jesus. We were all separated from God, which is the punishment for sin prescribed in scripture, and the issue was settled. Having been settled once and for all, it is eternally past. How do we know that it is past? The resurrection! Death is no more; life has replaced it once again. The Son of Man is forever the Son of God and lives unto the Creator of us all. And in that He lives, we also live unto God with and in Him. All of which is to say, our reconciliation is complete and secure, and death is gone forever.

Of course, I know what you are about to say. Will we not either grow old or have an accident or get sick and our days in the flesh end ? The answer is yes. What you are thinking and saying is absolutely true. It is natural, it is right, and it will happen. We shall go down to the dust, for it is the stuff from which we all came. No sweat! Big deal! So what? The only important thing is that we shall not die, it having happened once, never to happen again. We shall simply fall asleep and awake after God's likeness (image) in perfection, seeing clearly what before was like looking at a poor image in a mirror.

Believing this with all my heart, I share with you a wonderful joy. There is no fear in my life, at least not about the things of the Spirit. The seemingly big questions of where and what and when and why are no questions at all, and certainly there is no **if** concerning the matter. The sting of death is gone! I tell you it is so freeing not to constantly carry the fear of that moment when I must lay down my flesh's experience, what most of us call dying! I know the One who shall walk that moment with me for He is exists with/in me now, and He will on that day open the experience of life in its fullest to me. I fully appreciate why Paul wrote,

— *"For living to me means simply 'Christ,' and if I die I should merely gain more of Him. I realize, of course, that the work which I have started may make it necessary for me to go on living in this world. I should find it very hard to make a choice. I am torn in two directions—on the one hand I long to leave this world and live with Christ, and that is obviously the best thing for me. Yet, on the other hand, it is probably more necessary for you that I should stay here on earth."*[40]

What difference shall it ever make in terms of the big questions? In that we are alive to God now, never to have this relationship taken away, we shall certainly be alive to God forever, even into that new experience which takes us to the other side of the grave. What the prospect of that journey for me really is now, in the light of my faith, is the grandest adventure of all. I guess I look to that moment of passing from this life as akin to the moment just prior to walking into the church on the day I married my wife. My heart raced with excitement and anticipation, so much so that I wondered if I would get through the door. But when it opened and I saw her in all her radiant beauty, it was as if there was nothing else around me. No one else seemed to be there; my heart felt a calm that was pure peace. So it will be when I see God face to face. And, dear reader, see God clearly I shall, for He is my Father, my Eternal Creator, and Love has already written me into, and given me, the inheritance secured for us all in the Gospel of Jesus the Christ.

Your name is there, too.

Chapter Recap:

Death, biblically, means separation from God, not the end of days in the flesh. Disobedience was the cause of all humanity's separation from God; death was our common experience. God in redeeming love ordained that His creation, all of it, would be reconciled back to a right relationship with Him; would be given life again. This was done through the people Israel, specifically in the fullness of time in the man, Jesus, God with us, who died for us, that is, who took to himself the separation of us all and paid sin's penalty for us. Having now been paid, the penalty of death is no more and life with God is restored. It only remains for us to share the good news of what Jesus did, so that the sting of death can be let go and we all get on with the business of living and redeeming the world in His image.

CHAPTER THREE
SACRIFICE

Sacrifice is not an easy concept for twenty-first century people to deal with. We find it barbaric and cruel and relegate it to an age before we became civilized. Christian and non-Christian alike struggle with it in terms of its relationship to faith and consequently deal with it either as a good excuse not to be a believer or to relegate it to some pious, historical tradition far removed from anything meaningful to the present. It dawns on me in writing this that the reality of sacrifice in its ancient perspective is so far removed from us that sacrifice even in the little things of our time is a passing concept. How sad that we no longer are willing to sacrifice a little time for each other, a few dollars for the poor, or the present age for the life of those yet to come. Witness the national debt that will cripple future generations, so that we who now live can enjoy prosperity. Or witness the terrible misuse of the environment for the sake of present wealth at the expense of those who will inherit the deserts we shall leave behind.

Sacrifice is not a word used in our vocabulary. Yet, it is at the heart of the Good News and a calling upon those of every generation who are baptized into the life of Christ, those of us called to be his disciples and who have accepted the call to live just like him.

So, we examine the biblical meaning of sacrifice. Hold on to your chairs, for we are heading into waters that shall rock some boats and cause some yelling out to the man at the tiller. But do not worry. We are told that even in His resting, He is in charge.

A. We need to get a decent reference point for talking about sacrifice, one that starts and ends with our God as well as one that sets the pattern for what we personally are to experience in relationship to the concept. If sacrifice is to mean anything, it must first be something that is of the very nature of the God whom we are to image. Thinking thus, look with me to the seventeenth chapter of the Gospel of John. Here is what academics call the high priestly prayer of Jesus. It falls in the time-frame following the last Passover meal between Jesus and his disciples. The three Synoptic Gospels have Jesus going immediately to the garden called Gethsemane to pray after Judas' departure from the meal. John records a long discourse and then this great prayer contained as the entire seventeenth chapter.

There are several places in this chapter which give reference to God's giving of what is His to Jesus: verse 7, "...*all that you have given me comes from you,*" verse 10, "...*everything that is mine is yours and yours mine,*" verse 18, "...*just as you sent me into the world...,*" verse 22, "...*the honor that you gave me,*" ... and verse 24, "*Father, I want those whom you have given me....*" God is a giver. His desire is to give until all that He has fills the being of all that exists. Here, again, is the Genesis story in its inception, a description of a Creator who gives of His nature and Word to bring into being from nothing all that exists and who creates specifically a creature, man, who is to have the capacity to share His creativeness by the expression of his own will and the work of his own hands. We are, by His design, co-creators with God and re-creators of His own first work. Adam had this nature but his is a story of a simple, almost innocent disobedience. The great figures of the Old Covenant had this nature but theirs is a story of repeated wrong choice. Jesus had this nature and cherished it, nurtured it, increasing in wisdom and stature, and in favor with God and man. Here, in this Son, finally is found the vessel in which God's image and His alone shall be seen. The firstborn of all creation arrives.

Remember Moses' walk with God? It was pretty good by most any standard of measure; certainly he has got to be one of the giants of the family of faith. Remember while the Israelites were wandering around in the wilderness, Moses went up on the mountain to receive from God the peculiar code of conduct that would identify God's people in the midst of the world? Receiving the commandments of God, Moses came back down the mountain to be greeted by the people in worship before a golden calf (sort-of akin to a certain golden-tongued snake). In a rage, Moses rebuked the people, destroying in the process the stone tablets on which the laws were written, then having to return up the mountain to intercede once more with the Lord in behalf of this rebellious bunch. Exodus 33 lays out the full story. As Moses worked out what the relationship of God and the people was to be, he reminded God that it was in "going with us that we are distinct from all other people who are on the face of the earth." God acknowledged that such is indeed the truth, and then Moses said, "I pray thee, show me thy glory." A unique and unusual encounter unfolded, in which God showed Moses His back but not His face while His "glory passes by." Show me! Let me see you as you are! Then, maybe I, and we, can reflect your image! Show me.

I think that were I Moses, I would have considered that I had reached the ultimate, the pinnacle of honor and prestige, that I had finally seen it all. But, he had not. What he had experienced was certainly more than any other

24

mortal since the beginning, but God was not giving Himself to man again, remembering what had transpired with Adam. Not until the image could be restored at another tree would we see God giving Himself completely, giving His glory to His creation. Such was prophesied in Isaiah concerning the servant, Israel, when it was said,

— "*I am the Lord, that is my name; my glory I give to no other, nor my praise to graven images.*"[41]

Nonetheless, we must yet remember that God is a giver. He wills to, He exists for the purpose of, giving Himself away. As such, He, in Himself, sets the pattern for and the understanding of, sacrifice. In the act of creation, it was His Spirit moving on the face of the waters that brought all things into existence. It was His breath that caused man to become a living being. It was His word that went forth and created all that is out of that which was not. God caused the very existence of creation through the giving of Himself. It is in this sense that we must begin to understand the meaning of sacrifice.

It is small wonder that when the image of God is lost and the meaning of sacrifice corrupted, God separated humanity from Himself. God the giver is far removed from man the taker, now become so different both in spirit and in experience. Sacrifice as the experience of giving of self is foreign to the understanding of those more content to serve before idols through the giving of things. And it is in this latter sense that our history has nurtured the understanding of the term, sacrifice, and why it has become such an alien thought to so many. The giving of things, the giving of something outside of myself made by hands, even the giving of the life of another, that is sacrifice. However, do not ask me to give away me.

"Giving away all that is mine" is the heart and the Spirit of our God. It is just this that Jesus reveals to us in himself and which is the heart of his prayers to his Father:

— "*Everything that is mine is yours and yours mine... You gave me your glory... everything that is yours you gave to me... the love with which you have loved me... Abba.*"[42]

How is such shown to us? I would simply direct us to St. Paul, for it cannot be said any better.

— "*Let Christ Jesus be your example as to what your attitude should be. For he, who had always been God by nature, did not cling to his prerogatives as God's equal, but stripped himself of all privilege by consenting to be a slave by nature and being born as mortal man. And having become man, he humbled himself by living a life of utter obedience, even to the extent of dying, and the death he died was the death of a common criminal.*"[43]

God emptied Himself—of privilege, of distance, of power—He emptied Himself of self in order to make His life known to us in human form where we might see our own awesome, life-giving possibilities. God sacrificed Himself for us so that the image of Himself might be reflected in the sacrifices we make.

B. Let us look now more closely at the more traditional descriptions of sacrifice that come to us in the scriptures. Here we shall be talking about the sacrificial system of Israel that sets the stage for the Christ event. I speak of the sacrificial life of the temple and the role it plays for God's chosen people. The core of this is written in the legal code of Israel, the Torah or first five books of the Old Testament. Called the Pentateuch, also the law of Moses, the whole of Israel's cultic practice is portrayed in great detail, and sacrifice is the heart of it. The place of activity is the temple in Jerusalem; the main characters are the priests who oversee the rules of ritual and order. The high priest is the final participant before God in this sacred drama and to him is given the responsibility of maintaining and portraying the meaning of Israel's holy relationship with the Almighty.

In recognition that an entire book could be written trying to describe the wonderful drama and complexities of temple life, it must be sufficient for me merely to point you to the book of Leviticus and bid you to understand that in this present chapter of mine, I am neither attempting to definitively address sacrifice as a whole nor to embrace the vast intertwining of all that is encompassed by sacrifices, offerings, tithes and the specific reasons for each and every ritual. What I am seeking to do is to lead us to recognizing: 1) that the whole of Israel's life ebbs and flows around the cultic and ritual law and drama of temple life; and 2) that ultimately sacrifice and the shedding of blood is the climactic end of all that happens here between God and His people. If such can be accomplished, I trust that you will be encouraged by your own faith and desires to read and study more of what is contained in the Books of the Law.

In the Book of Leviticus, we find the story of the institution of a ceremony called the Day of Atonement. In chapters sixteen and seventeen, we find the Lord God talking to Moses after the death of the two sons of Aaron, describing the ceremony by which,

— *"atonement may be made for the people of Israel once in a year because of all their sins."*[44]

"Atonement: the means of becoming at one with; specifically, reconciliation of God and humanity; also, reparation for an offense or injury." This is the definition found in Webster's dictionary and is the burden of the rites given by God to Moses. When separation has occurred between two parties, how shall they be reunited in trust and love again? They are reconciled through atonement!

Thus was Moses now instructed. Two male goats were to be taken from the congregation of the people of Israel. They were to be similar in every respect so as to be seen with the eyes of faith as one animal. They were to be free of any blemish or fault, perfect in every way. Lots were to be cast over them so that one would be appointed for the Lord as a sin offering and the other designated as the scapegoat to be led away into the wilderness. The goat for the sin offering was to be killed for the people. Its blood was to be taken by the high priest within the veil of the Holy of Holies and sprinkled before the mercy seat and upon it. In so doing, the priest would make atonement for himself and for his house and for all the assembly of Israel. After finishing this atoning act, the priest was to take the second goat (yet representing one animal and a continuing action) and,

— *"...shall lay both his hands upon the head of the live goat and confess over him all the iniquities of the people of Israel, and all their transgressions, all their sins; and he shall put them upon the head of the goat, and shall send him away into the wilderness by the hand of a man who is in readiness. The goat shall bear all their iniquities upon him to a solitary land; and he shall let the goat go in the wilderness."*[45]

Leaving out some of the details of dress and protocol, this is the description of the chief redeeming act of the people of God under the Old Covenant. Once a year, every year, this sacrifice was to be offered and through it God and His people were brought near to each other again, no longer separated one from the other. How true the symbolism of the ritual is! God is in His eternal sanctuary (the holy of holies), seated upon His throne (the mercy seat of the Ark of the covenant), unapproachable in His glory (no one could enter the holy of holies except the high priest and he only once a year); mankind kept without, burdened with sin and iniquities, seeking God but unable to draw near because of disobedience. How should they be brought face to face again? The answer is: in the life (that is, in the blood) of one who is perfect in every way, without spot or blemish, without the taint of sin. The blood of the sacrifice is the means by which humankind approaches God and likewise the means by which God can behold His creation without compromising His own holiness.

Let me offer here a simple, spatial picture to help make this atoning act more personal. How shall we be one with someone whose image we have ceased to reflect, when we no longer look anything alike? How shall oneness be restored when we can neither deny the experiences that have shaped us nor return to a former moment to make a different choice? We are everything we have done, everything we have said, and everything we have thought—the accumulated product of our very existence—and nothing can change any part of it. We cannot return to the womb and get a second start nor can we end this life and be resurrected or reincarnated as different persons. We are what we are and the journey of life has left some blemishes and spots on us that keep us from looking like our Creator-God and bearing His image. We are thus separated from Him. Spatially, we describe it as God being in His heaven and we being of the earth, a wide gulf existing between us. In order for oneness to be restored, perfection (pure innocence) must somehow become ours, so that we reflect the perfection that is His. How? This way. The life of one who is perfect must be imputed, given, *"reckoned"*[46] to us. The life of one who is without blemish, one whose life is whole and holy in every way, whose journey from birth to the present has not been filled with choices or experiences or thoughts that have marred original innocence, needs to become our life. The life of this innocent, perfect one must be taken and that life given to us. His blood, *in which is his life*, must be put on us, given to us, become one with us! Then, when the Holy One who sits upon the throne of heaven, sees the blood, He sees only the perfection that is in the blood (the life) and, finding a perfect reflection of His own image, is one with that reflection, coming home in a perfect bond of peace. At-one! Atoned! Reconciled in a relationship that is now as it was originally created to be. It is a blessed and simple way, this way of the blood of the lamb in the act of the atonement.

And so the pattern was established for Israel by the grace of God, a pattern that allowed reconciliation to be made. "A statute for ever," so Leviticus 16 said. Sadly, this pattern is weakly glossed over by most of us in our contemporary spiritual life as we look at the sacrifice of Jesus. We forget that everything that happened at Calvary has its Old Covenant legal, liturgical, and prophetic precedent. The ritual of atonement was neither a flawed sacrifice nor an inefficient means of reconciling God and humanity to each other. Given and instituted by God, it was in every respect a complete and sufficient means of ridding the Covenant people of the taint and consequence of their sins, at least for the moment.

Noting this, we are then challenged to consider something that we heretofore might not have been willing to admit. It is this: if upon the completion of the sacrifice and the ridding of the scapegoat, the people of Israel were once again reconciled to their God and without sin, then we are brought to the place of having to say that innocence was restored and Israel, *at that moment*, was absolutely guiltless, sinless, in the presence of God. The people of God, the members of the house of Israel and participants in the Covenant established with Abraham and his seed forever, were restored to the perfection required of them and stood innocent and without sin. Interesting, isn't it? Leviticus 16:30 says,

— *"...for on this day shall atonement be made for you, to cleanse you; from all your sins you shall be clean before the Lord."*

And verse 34 adds,

— *"... that atonement may be made for the people of Israel once in the year because of all their sins."*

From *all* their sins, Israel was clean! Not just the high priest, or those in the city of Jerusalem, or those gathered at the temple for the ritual. No, Israel was clean by the act of that one high priest done once a year in the temple's holy of holies with the blood of the sacrifice. *All* were reconciled and not a single member of the Covenant community was left out.

Who was left out, then, of this wondrous experience? Only the gentiles. How were they ever to be reconciled? We will come to that later. For now, it is sufficient to know that for the immediate moments following the act of Atonement in the Temple, the people of God were without sin.

28

I have always found it interesting to ask Christians what they believe about the theology of repentance and forgiveness and the relationship of this sacrament to their own state of grace. What happens to us, in us, either through the forgiveness imparted us through the bishop or priest in worship following a general confession or through a more personal act of private confession in the *Book of Common Prayer* service called, "The Reconciliation of a Penitent?" What happens? Are we free from our sins? All of them? Are we then restored to innocence, at that very moment, for that moment? Are we then reconciled to God, made one with Him, and, at that moment and for that moment, restored to being a perfect image of the living God? Are we, then, at that moment, just like Jesus who was just like us in every way but without sin, perfect man? Usually in pursuing this, an affirmative answer to these questions starts out but then fades and stops as we push to the conclusion of being just like the savior, *the same as*. We are so afraid that if we say this about ourselves, we are either making ourselves to be more than we are or making Jesus to be less that he is, and fear causes us to back away from the only Good News that there is in the Gospel for us: new life in the fullness of the Spirit, the receiving of the promise of our Creator-God. How sad. We seem to prefer to wander in the wilderness rather than getting to the promised land.

But, back to Israel and our story of the atonement there. Sadly, corporate redemption for a people who have been asked corporately to be obedient lasted only but a moment. The next lie, the next theft, the next covetous glance by any member of the clans of Israel brought disobedience to the whole house and the need once again for the redeeming intercessions of the high priest when next year he entered the holy of holies.

C. We really should not go any further without paying a bit more attention to the idea of *blood* and the role it plays in Biblical life and the meaning it carries. Again, we must rely on the books of the law in the Old Testament and in particular, upon the book of Leviticus. The whole reason for sacrifice hinges on the shedding of blood. If this were not so, any offering could be made with the only characteristic probably being that it hold some sense of value to the one who makes the gift. Certainly in other rites of Israel and in the religious practices of the other peoples of the earth, offerings were given of food, of precious stones, of money, of human time, and of labor. In the Levitical writings, there were cereal offerings, wave offerings, tithes, and more. The stories of Israel told of various offerings and their reason and result. Witness the story of Cain and his offering from the produce of the land and the sweat of his labor. Note the offering of Hannah in the birth of Samuel and how he was given as a Nazarite even before he was conceived. Remember the observation of Jesus as he watched a woman offer her widow's mite at the treasury of the temple. All these were offerings of faith and value to the giver, but none either matched or took the place of the blood sacrifice as prescribed for the temple liturgy.

Leviticus 17:11 gives us the rationale for sacrifice and what meaning is ascribed to the blood that is offered:

— *"For the life of the flesh is in the blood; and I have given it for you upon the altar to make atonement for your souls; for it is that blood that makes atonement, by reason of the life."*[47]

We, of course, have no such understanding of the relationship between life and blood except the knowledge that one cannot live without it. We would be hard pressed to say where the life of the flesh is in our scientific world, for we can be clinically dead while technically alive. Our flesh can be kept warm, our lungs breathing, our heart beating, all through the use of machines. It is no longer simple enough to say that life is in the "whatever."

Yet, for our forebears in faith, the rule concerning blood and the definition of the role it played was very simple and very complete. God had said it and the people of God accepted it. Life was in the blood. Hence, the role it played in the liturgy of the temple was clear-cut. It was the power and essence behind the meaning of sacrifice. Blood was to be taken and offered and thus life, the life of the sacrificed creature, was to be placed before God.

This being true, then it makes sense to say that the animal or creature to be sacrificed ought to be perfect in every way. If the sacrifice was a goat or a bull or a lamb, it had to be without blemish. It was to be the very best animal of the flock, the most valuable beast of the herd. There was to be nothing offered that was either sick or crippled, nor could it be physically deformed or blemished. How clear was the exhortation in all of Israel's theology. The first-fruits, the firstborn, the first thoughts, the finest and best and most valued! I think about the tendencies of our own fallen thoughts and realize how we strive to always keep the best for ourselves and offer the leftovers to others. All too often our charity is the loose change from our pockets, our tithes and offerings that which is left over after we have paid the bills and planned our leisure, our aid to the poor the clothes that we no longer wear or want as we clean house to make room for the spring's new fashions. How contrary to the teaching of One who bids us,

— *"When you throw a party, invite those who can not repay you,"* and *"Take the lowest seat,"* and who praised the widow who . *"...gave all that she had, her very living."*[48]

Offer the lifeblood! No wonder it must be perfect, humbly taken from a perfect animal. There would be nothing offered to God which would be representative of the sin of His people who were in such need of redemption from the bonds of selfishness.

There is yet another Old Testament image of blood's power to save that must be mentioned. It is that of the memorial called the Passover. Israel's very being is fashioned on this one great moment of their history when the

God of their fathers rescued His people from the bonds of slavery to pharaoh in Egypt. The story of Moses and the Exodus is told and retold in the scriptures, found and rehearsed in the law, in the Psalms, and in the memories of the prophets.

— *"Remember, you were once slaves ...and God redeemed you with a mighty hand...."*[49]

The role of blood in this timeless story is found in the conclusion of Moses' confrontations with pharaoh when, after several failed attempts at persuading the Egyptian monarch to let the Hebrews go free, Moses proclaimed God's final act of witness to His authority over the creation: the sending forth of the angel of death to slay the firstborn of all living things. To prepare for what was about to be set in motion, Moses set forth some very specific instructions and in particular he described what was to be done to protect the lives of the firstborn of Israel:

— *"...on the tenth day of this month they shall take every man a lamb according to their father's houses, a lamb for a household; ...Your lamb shall be without blemish, a male a year old; ...they shall kill their lambs in the evening. And they shall take some of the blood, and put it on the two door posts and the lintel of the houses in which they eat them... It is the Lord's Passover. For I will pass through the land of Egypt that night, and I will smite all the firstborn of the land of Egypt, both man and beast; and on all the gods of Egypt I will execute judgments; I am the Lord. The blood will be a sign for you, upon the houses where you are; and when I see the blood, I will pass over you, and no plague shall fall upon you to destroy you, when I smite the land of Egypt... Then Moses said to them... For the Lord will pass through to slay the Egyptians; and when he sees the blood on the lintel and on the two door posts, the Lord will pass over the door, and not allow the destroyer to enter your houses to slay you."*[50]

Here, again, is the ancient imagery and pattern of a life that is blameless and without blemish, the perfect animal, whose blood (and life) is taken to be used as an offering and intercession for the people. Here, too, is the description of God seeing that life in the blood and recognizing His covenant-own and giving them passage from death to life with Himself. Who would not memorialize such an experience and relate it in feast and liturgy from generation to generation? Who would not set in law a prohibition on the use of blood for any purpose whatsoever except the holy expression of sacrificial loving?

— *"For the life of the flesh is in the blood; and I have given it for you upon the altar to make atonement for you souls; for it is the blood that makes atonement, by reason of the life."*[51]

D. Now, let us take sacrifice to its conclusion. Christians proclaim a crucified Christ whose life redeems the world from its sin. Much of humanity has found, and does find, the story a mystery, even repugnant, to the proclamation of a God who loves us in that experience. How can the death of someone, especially one proclaimed to be the firstborn Son of a loving Creator and Judge of all, reconcile us to the only Author of life? The Gospels tell us this story in fulfillment of the law and the prophets. We are told that God Himself will come to humanity as an Anointed One clothed in human flesh, to be all that humanity (and in particular, Israel) has been asked to be. He will come as a *"watchman"*[52] to sound clearly and loudly the clarion call of life to those who fail to see the enemy coming upon the gates. He will come as the *"shepherd"*[53] to seek, find, and lead the people safely back from the places of their bondage and wandering to the sheepfold of His care and safety where there is good pasture, clean water, and protection from the snare of the evil one. He will come as *"Israel, my servant"*[54] to fulfill all that is asked of God's covenant witnesses to the world. By this servant's life, innocence and holiness will be restored as the blessing to *"all the nations of the earth."*[55] He will be called Emmanuel (God is with us) and will be born of human flesh to a young woman. He will empty Himself of Godly powers to humbly take upon Himself the temptations of us all and live amongst us a life of witness to the holiness of God. Finally, He will bear in His own flesh the separation and death of all creation. All this God will do. This Anointed One's name will be Jesus (God saves) and it is he who will, *"save His people from their sins."*[56]

You either know or, I hope, will read the stories of Jesus' youth and of his ministry as an adult. I do not want to spend time here with them. I only remind us that they are written to claim and to convince us that Jesus is the promised Christ, this Anointed One from all eternity, who fulfilled what the prophets and rituals foretold. What I want us to examine here are those things related to our study concerning the use of blood, now to be portrayed in particular as his blood. It is the author of the Gospel of John to which we first turn and to his description of the aftermath of Jesus' feeding the multitudes with the fish and loaves. Following that experience, Jesus and his disciples left at evening time in a boat to cross the sea to Capernaum. The crowds awoke the next morning to find Jesus gone. Following him to the other side of the sea, they asked him when he had arrived. Jesus answered by saying that they sought after him for reasons not related to superficial things such as signs and wonders but rather for something that they did not understand, something related to the deepest hunger of us all, that being our reconciliation to our Creator and the hope of reclaiming once again our true humanity, that of His image.

— *"Do not labor for the food which perishes, but for the food which endures to eternal life which the Son of Man will give you... (for) he is the one who bears the stamp of God the Father."*[57]

I have used two translations here, the RSV and J. B. Phillips, to get the sense of this statement. Our hunger is for a life that reflects what is, that reflects the One who is, eternal. In the deepest recesses of our souls, at the foundation of our very selves, is the God-given desire to reflect the image of the Eternal One who gave us our life and who named us into being. It is most certainly a truth that we do not know how to articulate what has been so long lost in us and that therefore we most always seek for a substitute for what is our deepest hunger. No matter what we eat, we never find satisfaction and continue to seek something, anything (we know not what), in an endless, fruitless cycle.

— *"What must we do?... Believe in the one whom He has sent to you."*[58]

Believe in him; believe on him; believe as one with him. Become one with him and let him become one with you. All these ways of saying what the gospel writer has written convey the story that unfolds. It is a remembering of the Anointed One's description of how the life of one offered in innocence shall become the life of one tainted by disobedience. It is even related back to Moses!

— *"...but what matters is not that Moses gave you bread to eat from heaven but that my Father is giving you the true bread from heaven. For the bread of God which comes down from heaven gives life to the world."*[59]

Gives *life*! Gives reconciliation! Ends separation! Ends *death*! Makes humanity in the image of his Creator again! Jesus then says,

— *"I myself am the bread of life... Unless you do eat the body of the Son of Man and drink his blood, you are not living at all. The man who eats my flesh and drinks my blood has eternal life... my body is real food and my blood is real drink. The man who eats my body and drinks my blood shares my life and I share his. Just as the living Father sent me and I am alive because of the Father, so the man who lives on me will live because of me."*[60]

The gospeler writes that those who heard this from Jesus said,

— *"This is a hard teaching indeed; who could accept that?"*[61]

It is not a hard saying! It is the clearest, simplest truth one can find! Jesus is describing the plan hidden, if you will, from the soul by the hardness of the sinful heart. God wants us to have His image and will even ensure that we are dressed in it by clothing us Himself with Himself.

— *"It is the Spirit which gives life. The flesh will not help you."*[62]

God does it for us, to us, in us. We have not the faintest idea of what is holy, let alone how to be holy. No one has ever witnessed to us pure and consistent holiness for us to see and to make our own! History's witness up to the advent of this Son of Man reflects the truth of what the scriptures say,

— *"Everyone has sinned, everyone falls short of the beauty of God's plan."*[63]

God comes and does in our flesh, for our flesh, what He has eternally willed. He gives us life by giving us His blood.

Then the end comes for the Anointed One's witness. Jesus tried to prepare his disciples for it. He told them plainly what was coming, his passion in Jerusalem, and why it must not be circumvented. They did not want to hear it. How much easier, more acceptable, it would be to try to alter the image of Love, for that is humanity's choice. Peter said it must not happen to the Master and ultimately tried to alter it with a sword. Poor image! James and John thought a lot about the words of the Master and the kingdom they would inherit with him and asked to be chief amongst the authorities in it. Poor image! Judas thought there should be another way, a better way, and if the Master would not choose it, he would make it happen with a little help from the authorities. Poor image! These are but some of the examples of how badly they, and we, miss the message of the Spirit. The image of the Eternal One must be solely and simply that: the image of the Creator. It had been circumvented, replaced, compromised, denied for too long and now One had come to make it known even unto death, death on a cross. The tempter would even be allowed his one, last, opportune time. So, Jesus continued to prepare, to teach, to show the way, its truth, and his life to his chosen followers until the end.

On the night in which he was betrayed, he gathered his disciples in a room prepared for them to celebrate together the Passover meal. Remember, now, what we have already observed about this idea of Passover. When they had gathered themselves around the table, Jesus began the meal. In it, he did something new, different, for when he took the bread to pass amongst them, he first gave thanks to God and then told them,

— *"This bread is my body which is being broken for you. Do this in remembrance of me."*[64]

The lamb (the goat of the atonement) must die, its body broken for the people. Even the high priest earlier that fateful year observed this before his peers when he said,

— *"You do not realize that it would be a good thing for us if one man should die for the sake of the people—instead of the whole nation being destroyed."*[65]

The gospeler then writes,

— *"(He did not make this remark on his own initiative but, since he was high priest that year, he was in fact inspired to say that Jesus was going to die for the nation's sake—and in fact not for the nation only, but to bring together into one family all the children of God scattered throughout the world.)"*[66]

Then Jesus took a cup filled with wine, and after thanking God, he gave it to them with the words,

— *"Drink this, all of you, for it is my blood, the blood of the new agreement shed to set many free from their sins."*[67]

This is my blood! As part of a Passover meal, Jesus said the wine is his blood to set one free from the bondage that holds one to sin and its separation (death). It is the covering over the *house* of our bodies. As a reference to the rite of the atonement, it is the blood of the lamb applied to the corners of the mercy seat that shelters the throne of God residing in our hearts. Being the blood of the Anointed One, this cup of blessing is the life offered by and through which the living God of the universe shall see His creation and behold only its innocence and holiness.

Now we can begin to get some understanding of the "Why?" of his obedience, even to betrayal, trial, and the ugly agony of the passion and the cross. Innocence could still be lost and obedience and holiness compromised. To fight, to hide, to deny or debate, would destroy the image of Love and the glory of his Father. To argue and curse, to accuse and condemn, would mirror the father of lies and the author of separation (death). The only way was to continue to be who he was born to be. Pilate asked him at his trial, "*Who are you?*" He uttered not a word. Another account has him saying in response to the question as to whether or not he was a king, "*You say that I am.*" I believe that both in his silent Spirit and in his short answer he is telling the holy truth of it all: "I am who I am." **I AM**!

— "*Tell them I AM sent you.*"[68]

From his beaten body, from the lacerations of the thorns that crowned his head, from the wounds of the nails that held him to the tree and the final insult of the spear that pierced his side, poured forth the blood that was offered for his disciples, filled the cup of the Passover for the forgiveness of sin, and covered the earth that held his cross. This blood would eternally cry out in intercession for the children of the Father of all. And everywhere that God would look from that moment, He would see the blood and be well pleased with the image of innocence reflected back, and He would draw near and therein dwell. At-one.

Some final observations as we come to the end of this chapter on sacrifice are in order. Remember that it is God who is at work in all of this. It is the Creator whose image is holy and pure and who seeks to be one with His creation in holiness' glory. When the creation fails and falls, it is God the Creator who works out its salvation. It is God who establishes the work of the Atonement in the sacrament of sacrifice and blood. It is God who calls forth the intercessions of the high priest and the singular work that redeems the people in the Holy of Holies. Then remember that at the right time, it is the Creator-God who declares that the work of holiness asked of a covenant people shall be accomplished by His own hand and work as He clothes Himself with the flesh of humanity and draws near as the shepherd of souls, the watchman of our lives, the servant who suffers for all as a lamb led to the sacrifice. He is the child whom the angel says is Immanuel, God with us, who saves the people from their sins. God is the Son of Man grown wise and mature who reveals in human actions and words God's life in an image such as to allow the claim,

— "*If you see me, you see the Father. He and I are one.*"[69]

Finally, remember that it is the Creator clothed in the very limitations of the flesh of His creation that goes even to death on a cross. There, He reveals His Love and glory completely so that Love's image can be restored in us. Through His blood, God makes all of us one with Himself now and forever, atoned and redeemed. God saves (it is what the name, Jesus, means)! Surely,

35

it is the name that is above every name! It is the very word that reflects the totality of Love's best story and a name that recalls the very life we can live. To that name every weak and fallen knee in our hearts can bow and find healing and new life, and nothing under all of heaven or in all the earth can stop us from revealing the image that cries out from the very dust of our flesh. Jesus, Christ of Glory; Christ in us, hope of glory; one life together in whom the Father is seen and made known.

CHAPTER RECAP:

Sacrifice is at the very heart of the image of God for it reflects the eternal giving that brings forth life and the creation of all things. God gave of Himself to bring into being from nothing all that exists. It is also to be the image of the life of all created things who, reflecting their Creator, are to offer themselves for one another and the stewardship of the universe.

When the image was lost, God declared that the sacrifice of a life, and the element of blood in which is the life of that which is sacrificed, should be made for the purpose of atoning the whole creation back to Him again. Through the death of an animal that is perfect and without deforming blemish, and through the offering of the blood of this one who is slain at the holy of holies, God shall see His people and they and He shall be made one, atoned, again. Jesus is the lamb of God that is slain, whose blood sets humanity free.

He is both priest and victim, the one who offers the blood and intercedes in our behalf *and* the sacrifice who dies and sheds the blood used in the holy of holies. The blood that he offers at his death on the cross is his own and is shared with us forever in the sacrament of bread and wine at the supper which honors his name. Sacrifice is the way, the truth, and the life of all creation.

CHAPTER FOUR
THE CHRIST

You are by now aware that everything we are doing with this work pushes us to the historical experience of the man, Jesus. The Christian faith sees him as the fulfillment of the Old Covenant, the perfect image of the law and the words of the prophets, and marks the movement of history, so as to reflect the idea that what existed before him led to the necessity of his appearing and that what exists in the present is at its fullest when it reflects his life. It is all related to the idea of image and Christian people commit themselves to living as disciples of Jesus as the surest way of living out the inheritance for which humanity was originally created.

From the story we are following—the old covenant experience of Israel—comes the description of one who was expected by the prophets, one who was called the Anointed One, the Messiah. References to his appearing are many: some direct and specific such as from the prophets, others probably read into the sacred literature by the authors of the new covenant and by contemporary theologians who see with their own mind's eye things that feel like this One whom we call Lord. There is no doubt that Isaiah refers to this future man of God in talking about the true Israel, the man who shall bear suffering not only for the tribes of Jacob but as a light to the nations. Ezekiel's great shepherd passage concerning God's own work to keep his flock; Jeremiah's righteous branch from David's lineage; Zechariah's humble king who comes on the colt, the foal of an ass: all say the same with great clarity and hope and are unmistakable to the person of faith—God's Anointed One who shall restore the kingdom of heaven to us! The Anointed One of God is also translated as Messiah, also as Christ. We are talking of the same figure in scripture who is described as the Son of God, God incarnate (Emmanuel). Let us then spend some time getting to know this man and the specific figure of the Christ. His name is Jesus.

A. When was the presence of God, Love's image, seen in humanity? Was it ever there or was it merely the story of what was meant to be "in the beginning?" The answers will never be known except to the heart of faith and to that heart comes the conviction that what once surely should have been, might have been, will finally come forth; it is the will of God our Creator. That heart has been the life of the Old Covenant people since Abraham. It is voiced in thoughts of longing for God's presence with us, a presence that restores innocence and brings paradise back in our midst. It cries out from the loneliness of human souls and acknowledges the awful reality of endless days and nights feeling empty, separated from the comfort and embrace of a Love that reaches to the depths of our existence. We cry,

— *"Who are You and where do You dwell; I want to know You? Who am I and why do I feel far from You and always so afraid?"*

All cultures deal with these thoughts of human longings and all wrap such longings in the shrouds of myths and allegories that try to proclaim the Spirit's truth. But with the history of the people called Israel, come proclamations of a prophetic figure that grew out of the longing for oneness with their covenant God, proclamations believed upon as promises of God made known through the unique persons of the prophets. This Anointed One who would come would live out in his flesh the image of the Creator's holiness and in so doing would open again the way to paradise, restoring the relationship of innocence and life to us all.

I think that the first best attempt at showing the life of God in human flesh (after Abraham's great witness to obedience at the sacrificial offering of his son, Isaac) came with the proclamation by Moses of the unique law received from God and presented to the people in the midst of their exodus from slavery in Egypt. Israel's code of conduct, the Ten Commandments, a law that would be so special a witness before the nations of the world that they, the Gentiles, would want to come to this way of living as well, became for this people a promise, a covenanted way of living, with their God:

— *"We will be your people and you will be our God, for the whole earth is yours. We will be for you in the midst of the earth a holy nation, a kingdom of priest's, your own people."* [70]

Four commandments for knowing and living in a relationship with our Creator and six commandments for knowing and living in loving relationships with our neighbors were presented to the whole nation and as a body they agreed to live under the authority of these laws:

— *"This we will do!"* [71]

Herein was to be seen the power of God's redeeming love. By living in accordance with these commandments, this body of people, the seed of Abraham who were committed to be God's blessing to the whole earth, would show forth the very nature of God and restore to humanity the image of life that is the reflection of all that is eternal. Paradise, the visual realm of

38

God, would be reclaimed on the earth and God Himself would come and rule in love amongst His creation. All of the nations would see and come to be transformed by the beauty of these laws and the life they create. Sin and darkness would end, humanity's divisions and hatreds would cease, death would be no more, and love would be the bond that would unite us all as the children of God.

It is a good plan. However, Moses never even got the sacred law into the hands of the people before they had reverted to their old gods and to their old ways. And though Moses kept the people in the wilderness for forty years in order to bring a new generation up in the ways of these laws, never was there a season or a time that made known the way of life decreed in such a way as to make visible the generous grace of God. The history of Israel written in the book of Judges records failure upon failure:

— *"And the people of Israel did what was evil in the sight of the Lord, forgetting the Lord their God and serving the Baals and the Asheroth."*[73]

Peasant and priest alike stumble. And all the time, God remained the hidden one, distanced from the disobedience of a people that marred His image, coming only in mystery to the holiness of the tabernacle in Israel's midst and to the sacred ark of the covenant that resides within it. There he remained connected by His covenant promise, and in the holiness of worship continued to work out His will.

In time, the people were gathered as a nation into the expression of a kingdom under a temporal ruler and one came to the throne who addressed the reality of God's presence in their midst and how His presence is expressed. David, the great king who united the people and raised the nation to grandeur, spoke of his embarrassment that while he lived in a large and gracious home of cedar, *"...the ark of God dwells in a tent."* He proclaimed that he would build God a home fitting for His presence. A prophet by the name of Nathan brought David the word of the Lord that came to him in the night and said that God had other plans. Rather than having David build a house, the prophet was to say,

— *"... the Lord declares to you that the Lord will make you a house... I will raise up your offspring after you, who shall come forth from your body, and I will establish his kingdom for ever. I will be his father, and he shall be my son... I will not take my steadfast love from him... your throne shall be established for ever."*[74]

How interesting this word from the prophet is and how widely it has been interpreted. The usual interpretation has been that a forthcoming heir and son from the lineage of David would construct and build a home for God, a temple for His worship and in which His presence would dwell. Solomon, king after David, received this word just that way and constructed the first great temple in Jerusalem and God had a home. Through the centuries, two great temples were built on Jerusalem's holy mount, the process finally ending with the violent destruction of both city and temple by the Romans in AD 70. Now again in our day, Jews and Christians alike look to this and other words of the scriptures to proclaim the necessity of building yet again a great temple as a dwelling place for God, a manifestation of His image and holiness and the affirmation of His ultimate authority and presence. But please give prayerful consideration to the reality of this interpretation: the God of Love and Prince of Peace claiming a home of wood and stone with which to show forth His image in the midst of the most violence-prone and blood-soaked site on earth. For mind you, that is what history already records for Jerusalem's temple mount, and it is surely what will be witnessed if Jew and Moslem vie for control and whether the Moslem holy place called the *Dome of the Rock* or the Jewish holy place called *The Temple* shall exist there.

From the beginning of the interpretations of Nathan's word for David, pain and struggle have resulted from thinking that wood and stone shall show forth God's image and presence. Solomon's interpretation and construction early laid the seeds of pain and division for the nation as the people revolted after his death, engaging in civil war over the taxation and bond-slavery required to finance and raise his many grand buildings, of which the temple to God was foremost.

It must try God's patience immensely. Think of all the places and things we human beings have declared holy to the image of gods (and our God) down through the ages and the resultant violence perpetrated to defend and/or rescue the same. The crusades of the middle ages come foremost to mind. Even into these early years of the twenty-first century, a time when we like to think we are more educated and rational, Hindus and Moslems in India kill each other for control of land that is holy to both while out of the same rationale violence has raged for years for land that is to be Protestant or Catholic in Northern Ireland, Christian or Moslem in Serbia and the Sudan. Looking at the utter devastation to land and humanity that results from such interpretations, one can only wonder of the nature, the image, that is portrayed to our neighbors of the God or gods that we assign to such holiness. Surely, the image shown cannot be the God of our fathers or of our Lord, Jesus, nor can such interpretation give glory to His Name.

Let us look at Nathan's prophecy to David in another way. Let us read and receive the word of the Lord as the Revised Standard Version (RSV) translates it and take it at face value:

— *"Moreover the Lord declares to **you** that the Lord will make **you** a house."*

I have highlighted the pronouns so that they can be read there with emphasis. God will make **you**, David, the house of God, the place of His abiding and the expression of His glory. The flesh of David, the man, was the place where God would dwell and out of his flesh, from his seed, his offspring, would come forth the house, the temple of God's presence that would last forever, one who would build in his own flesh the obedient witness to God that would be seen as the fullness of glory. Seen this way, Solomon missed the mark terribly as did successive generations. Seen in this way, so does the majority of our humanity today miss the mark.

But, back to the temple built by Solomon and the witness that unfolded there with the Hebrews to Israel's covenant with God. It, at least, became the place where the ordinances governing Israel's worship of God were carried out. There, sacrifices of every sort were offered according to the Levitical law and there the most holy rite of the Atonement was performed year after year. What God had asked of His people was carried out. But something happened over time that reflected the continual misinterpretation of making *things* holy. Those who came to offer sacrifice and those who worked to do the sacrifice, peasant and priest alike, got drawn into the shadow-life of thinking that being there, in the temple, fulfilled what is asked of humanity by God, that doing it, the sacrifice, made them holy. They did not understand (and for the most part, we do not, either) that when the will of God for humanity gets externalized and focused on something outside ourselves in such a way as to seek to fulfill the requirement of the written law without ever really making sacrifice of self the way of life, we fail and become disobedient instead. How might I drive this home?

— *"Do not trust in these deceptive words: 'This is the temple of the Lord, the temple of the Lord, the temple of the Lord.' ... Behold, you trust in deceptive words to no avail. Will you steal, murder, commit adultery, swear falsely, burn incense to Baal... and then come and stand before me in this house, which is called by my name, and say, 'We are delivered!!'—only to go on doing all these things?"*[5]—Jeremiah

— *"With what shall I come before the Lord, and bow myself before God on high? Shall I come before him with burnt offerings, with calves a year old?... He has showed you, O man, what is good; and what does the Lord require of you but to do justice, and to love kindness, and to walk humbly with your God?"*[6] —Micah

— *"For I desire steadfast love and not sacrifice, the knowledge of God, rather than burnt offerings."*[7] —Hosea

Maybe that's enough for now. I could also refer to the gospels where Jesus confronts the religious authorities with the famous "Woe to you" passages, but we must press on here in search of the Christ. As Israel's history unfolded in chaos and war, something interesting began to happen in the covenant arena of what God required from Israel. From Abraham to Moses, Israel, as a people, a nation, covenanted to show forth the image of God through obedience to His commands. But, as they repeatedly failed at it from generation to generation, another word sprang forth that spoke of obedience from only some within the covenant family. Through the prophets came a word portraying a work of God that would rise up from amongst disobedient Israel a remnant of the people who would return to the spirit of the covenant made with the Almighty and who would live Israel's sacred promises with honesty and integrity. Isaiah, Jeremiah, Micah, Zachariah: all speak of a time coming when a remnant would return, or a remnant be raised up in Israel who would bear the image of holiness. From all of the people, now to a remnant: bearers of God's glory.

It is almost as if the story of Abraham's intercessions for Sodom and Gomorrah got relived in Israel's history. In that story, Abraham and God were talking about God's decision to destroy the cities because of their sinfulness. Abraham drew near to God and said,

— *"Will you indeed destroy the righteous with the wicked? Suppose there are fifty righteous within the city?"... And the Lord said, "If I find at Sodom fifty righteous in the city, I will spare the whole place for their sake."... "Suppose five of the fifty righteous are lacking? Will you destroy the whole city for lack of five?"... God said, "I will not destroy it if I find forty-five there."... "Suppose forty are found there?... Suppose thirty?... Suppose twenty?... Suppose ten?"... And the Lord answered, "For the sake of ten I will not destroy it."*[78]

Such an honest exchange in a marvelous relationship between Abraham and his God!

God would use a remnant for the sake of seeing Israel fulfill her ancient and sacred covenant made first with Abraham and renewed through all the generations down into the midst of Israel's life as a divided nation. If but a remnant would return literally and spiritually, living in the bonds of righteousness and justice, showing forth mercy and compassion, living from the heart what was portrayed outwardly in worship, the Lord God would draw near, restore paradise and renew His creation. For it was in the people, in their relationships with one another that show forth their covenant laws, that the Eternal One's image must be seen and His work of creation and re-creation poured forth. And all that it would take to show this was a remnant; maybe fifty, maybe twenty, maybe....

B. But in truth, even the remnant would fail and the work of God would come down to one righteous man. Israel called him the Anointed One, the Messiah. To him we now look. References to his appearing are many. I remind us of Nathan's words to David; "I will raise up your **offspring**... and I will establish **his** kingdom." Offspring. His. The Anointed One. Isaiah told the people that in the time of their greatest troubles, though only a remnant remain like an oak that also finally falls, when the tree is felled,

— *"The holy seed is its stump... There shall come forth a shoot from the stump of Jesse, and a branch shall grow out of its roots... the root of Jesse shall stand as an ensign to the peoples; him shall the nations seek."*[79] The Messiah.

Also, Micah proclaimed,

— *"But you, O Bethlehem Ephrathah, who are little to be among the clans of*

Judah, from you shall come forth for me one who is to be ruler in Israel, whose origin is from old, from ancient days."[80] The Messiah.

Jeremiah added,

— *"Behold the days are coming, says the Lord, when I will raise up for David a righteous Branch, and he shall reign as king and deal wisely, and shall execute justice and righteousness in the land. In his days, Judah will be saved and Israel will dwell securely. And this is the name by which he will be called: The Lord is our righteousness."*[81] The Messiah.

Ezekiel described God's own work of shepherding and redeeming His flock in this way:

— *"And I will set over them one shepherd, my servant David, and he shall feed them: he shall feed them and be their shepherd. And I, the Lord, will be their God, and my servant David shall be prince among them; I, the Lord, have spoken."*[82] The Messiah.

Even the earliest stories can become a herald of this message and of One who holds forth God's glory. To the serpent of Genesis, God said,

— *"I will put enmity between you and the woman, and between your seed and her seed; he shall bruise your head, and you shall bruise his heel."*[83] The Messiah.

The person of the Messiah is the expression of Israel's final hope, arising most dramatically in the messages of those charismatic figures, the prophets, whose appearing coincided with times of travail and confusion in national life. Be it the result of sin and disobedience from within or the threat and presence of destruction from without, as the people withered under the weight of their afflictions, the voice of the prophet heralded the will of God whose commitment to the ancient covenant and adherence to His own holiness would ultimately prevail and see to the restoration of His people. The Lord would come and His reign over Israel would establish His kingdom amongst them and the peoples of all the earth. He would gather the victory with His own right arm and all the enemy would be put to flight. How glorious this must have sounded to a people struggling, in exile, in the depths of despair.

It is no wonder that at every juncture of the history of this covenant people, the thought of their oppressor's defeat, the rebuilding of their own homeland and society under a Davidic king, and the restoration of a land at peace and as rich and grand as any on the earth would be a constant and consistent thought. Such an appearance and coming of the Messiah was the truth for most all the Old Covenant's people, the truth for most all the New Covenant's people, and remains the truth for most Christians in the twenty-first century. An earthly kingdom, the best and final expression of all the kingdoms upon earth, the final and surest reign of an eternal king whose victory is over all authority in heaven and on earth: this, seemingly, is what everyone awaits! But the political, geographical kingdom is not the covenant truth that God has proclaimed, rather only a shadow of it. The Messiah's kingdom is not of this world!

C. The Anointed One is the Messiah. The Messiah is the Christ. The Christ is the Anointed One who is *the image of the invisible God* and the One who *reflects the glory of God and bears the very stamp of his nature.*[84] It is to this that we have been moving. We obviously have been and are talking about one and the same figure and have been using the story of Israel to demonstrate his appearing and the place he fills in God's plan of salvation.

I feel it necessary to remind us as we come near to the end of this chapter of where we are going and the flow of this journey. The biblical drama is a story of God's restoration of His creation, and humanity in particular, to the perfect reflection of His own nature. Having lost this image somehow, somewhere, in the long ago, we, and the rest of creation, had been bound in death; we died when separation from our Creator became the consequence of our forefathers disobedience. God, being true to His own nature, went immediately about the work of restoring us to life, to a reconciled relationship with Himself that restores in us a true and perfect image of Himself and a living, practiced presentation of His Love in all our relationships. It is the Christ who came to fulfill this work and to show the image of God that is meant to be seen in all humanity.

Now, let us get on. In the fullness of time, Christ was born. This phrase—in the fullness of time—has been like a beacon for me ever since I first saw its use and place in the study called the *Bethel Series*, authored by The Rev. Harley Swiggum and made available through the Adult Christian Education Foundation in Madison, Wisconsin. In the fullness of time, Christ! The drama of Israel had run full to the climax for which the nation existed, that climax being the Anointed One's appearing.

According to all that was prepared and expected, God came down. What a beautiful way to describe the union of the eternal and the finite, Spirit and flesh, God and man! However, being no longer tied to the ancient or medieval cosmology, it is now better described simply as, God came. His coming was witnessed in the birth of a human baby, a boy, to a woman whose name was Mary. She was the betrothed of Joseph of the house of David. It is a story you know well! But look closely with me to certain parts of it. From three gospels (Matthew, Luke and John) comes these words about what was conceived in Mary's womb:[85]

— The child, a son, was *of the Holy Spirit,* was *with God and was God and existed with God from the beginning* when *God expressed himself.* I am appreciative of J.B. Phillips' translation of the prologue of John's gospel: *At the beginning God expressed himself.* He created man in the beginning as the image of Himself because even before anything existed, it was eternally Love's nature to express itself. Now, in this moment of the fullness of time, the Creator clothes Himself in Mary's womb with the flesh of *her* nature as He expresses Himself in the flesh by the eternal Spirit of *His* nature.

— *"you shall call his name, Jesus,"* which fulfilled Isaiah's prophecy, *"that his name shall be called Emanuel."* Jesus, which means Yahweh (or God) saves; Emmanuel, which means God with us: both of these names bear the power of the thought that it is God at work, God in this historical moment, God doing what is needful of being accomplished, God making Himself known in finite flesh, God's image that will be seen amongst us full of grace and truth! God is come!

— *"In him appeared life and this life was the light of the world."* Life appeared when there had only existed death. Life, as being the light of God, as being in union with or in a relationship with the Creator, as being the glory of God, as being the image of God! Life that is the holiness and the righteousness and the justice and the love of God. He, this child that is born, appeared to make the life of God, like light, known; to shine, as it were, upon all children as they come into the world so that every one who is born of the flesh might also grow and live in that same perfect relationship of oneness with God.

— *"...the Lord God will give to him the throne of his father David...and of his kingdom there will be no end."* This child was of the flesh of David, the temple figure of the ancient prophecy of Nathan, "I will make you a temple." Here was the temple of God, this infant child of Mary's womb. Here was the place where God dwelt and made Himself known to all flesh. Here was the one, true, holy place; this, a temple of the eternal and everlasting Spirit that had always been and that will never end.

— *"...there is a grace in our lives because of his grace. For while the law was given by Moses, love and truth came through Jesus Christ. It is true that no one has ever seen God at any time. Yet the divine and only Son, who lives in the closest intimacy with the Father, has made him known."* This is absolutely a perfect statement about the plan of God to witness in His creation His own image and to restore it when the first creation fell into the reflection of another!

How was it, by chance or by grace, that Mary and Joseph were chosen to be the earthly parents and guardians of the Anointed One? That they were the right choice, the unfolding life of the child proved. How important for the life of the flesh our parents are! Children image; it is how they grow and become! It is a process that has no equal and there is no avoidance of its unfolding work. Children become what they see and hear of their environment and pattern the experiences of their earliest memory. It even occurs in the developmental time of the womb by response to the emotions of the mother and the sounds that are transmitted through her flesh. Describing this in the animal world, we call it imprinting. It is no less a description of what the human animal goes through. And though it is certainly true that some children become the opposite of what their parental expression is—bad children from good parents, good children from bad parents—the process holds true most generally in all societies and in all times. We reflect and participate in the spirits of the lives of those with whom we are a common life and flesh. One need only read the news or observe the community in which one lives to see the reflection or prejudices of one generation passed directly on to the next: racial, spiritual, social, economic, educational lifestyles repeated from parent to child.

It seems right in my heart to assume that what Matthew and Luke in particular portrayed of the infancy of Jesus most likely was an accurate description of the spirit of the parental relationship of Mary and Joseph to their child. For Jesus to be the Anointed One bearing in his flesh the image of the invisible God, he would have had to know this from the beginning of his flesh. I can, therefore, envision Mary and Joseph talking of her pregnancy with the awe and mystery of new life developing in Mary's womb in such terms as,

— *"It is a miracle! Our God has visited me and given into me the Child of His Love. Our baby will be holy, the glory of the Almighty One."*

More so, it is a wondrous gift for a mother to love what is created at conception as much as that which is revealed at birth, and to nurture that which is developing as fully as that which is nourished in infancy:

— *"Little one who is safe within, Angels spoke of your coming into me and angels will rejoice in your coming into the world. All people everywhere will adore you as much as I do and will look to you even as I will fill my eyes with your beauty."*

I believe that Mary sang songs of peace to her unborn son and Joseph spoke words of love to mother and child alike. And as he grew from infancy to being a young child and on into the years of youth and adult, I think that Jesus saw in Mary and Joseph a holy and intimate love and spirit and heard always in their conversations about him and with him and in his presence those things that reflected their knowledge of the Almighty's presence in their lives, their covenant understanding of Israel's life, and their confidence that this child of theirs was the expected Messiah, God's Anointed, who would save the people from their sin. I know they must have said often how deeply pleased they were with this, their dearly-loved son. Proud and loving parents do that! They called him, Emmanuel; he was the salvation miracle of God—Jesus.

— *"The child grew up and became strong and full of wisdom. And God's blessing was upon him."*[86]

Let us look now to how the gospels unfold this witness and see if we can find in their words the image of God that they saw reflected in human flesh.

There was a man by the name of Simeon to whom it had been revealed that he would not die before he saw the Lord's Christ. *"... At last, Lord, you can dismiss your servant in peace, as you promised! For with my own eyes I have **seen** your salvation which you have made ready for every people... a light to **show** truth to the Gentiles and bring glory to your people Israel."*[87]

46

There was a man by the name of John, called the Baptist, who cried out, *'You must change your hearts... for the kingdom of Heaven has arrived!'* To the Pharisees and Sadducees coming for baptism he said, *'Go and do something to show that your hearts are really changed!'* When Jesus came to him to be baptized, John tried to prevent him. *'I need you to baptize me. Surely you do not come to me?'* Jesus replied, *'It is right for us to meet all the Law's demands—let it be so now.'* Then John agreed to the baptism. Jesus came up out of the water, the heavens opened and the Spirit of God came down like a dove and rested on him, and a voice out of Heaven came, *'This is my dearly-beloved Son, in whom I am well pleased.'*[88]

Jesus immediately found himself in a time of temptation about who he was. He felt the aloneness of it; it was a wild and strange place for him. Fasting and praying, temptation beset him about his life and who he was. Over and over again, the tempter of his soul said, *"If you really are the Son of God...change stones...throw yourself from the high ledge of God's house...worship me!"*[89] If you are the Son of God! *If!* Such awful, powerful, tempting, misleading words to hear! They raise up within the soul the doubts and questions of all humanity going way back, I suspect, to the beginnings when stories were told of another experience of temptation in a perfect garden with one who was innocent but less secure in who she was. Jesus, too, is so tempted. *"If? Who am I? I have been told for as long as I can remember that I am the son of my Father in heaven. And I, myself, have heard His voice speaking to me. I am my Father's son. I am. I am who I am. I AM."* Then the devil let him alone until a more opportune time and angels came to him and took care of him.

Jesus returned from this experience in the power of the Spirit and came to Nazareth and went to the synagogue on the Sabbath. There, he stood up to read the scriptures and the book of the prophet Isaiah was handed to him. He began to read, *"The Spirit of the Lord is upon me. He has anointed me...."* He shut the book. *Every eye was fixed upon him!* He said, *"This very day this scripture has been fulfilled, while you have been listening to it!"*[90] The Anointed One. The people **saw** him as they listened to him read in their presence.

Jesus called to himself those to whom he would first reveal himself, teach how to live and share the life of paradise, and disciple into the image of his Father in order to complete the redemption of the world. Several were first John the Baptist's disciples who heard John say, *"Look, there is the lamb of God who will take away the sin of the world!.. I have seen the Spirit come down like a dove from Heaven and rest upon him...he who sent me to baptize told me: 'The one on whom you will see the Spirit coming down and resting is the man who baptizes with the Holy Spirit!' Now I have seen this happen and I declare publicly before you that he is the Son of God!"*[91] The Anointed One! One who came to Jesus through John's witness to his disciples was Nathaniel. Jesus told him and the others, *"I tell you all that you will see Heaven wide open and God's angels ascending and descending around the Son of Man!"*[92]

Over and over we hear the testimony of those who witnessed in this man something new that aroused in their hearts a hunger for what he himself had. A woman at a well shared a drink of water and a conversation with him that finally led her to say,

— *"I know that Messiah is coming, you know, the one who is called Christ. When he comes he will make everything plain to us."*

"I am Christ speaking to you now," said Jesus.

It so touched a thirst in her that she ran home to her kinsfolk and said to them,

— *"Come and see the man who told me everything I've ever done! Can this be Christ?"* After they followed and listened to him, they finally made this statement, *"We don't believe any more now because of what you said. We have heard him with our own ears. We know that this must be the man who will save the world."*[3]

Later, after healing a lame man who could not get to the Pool of Bethzatha near the sheep-gate fast enough for his healing when an angel came to move the waters, Jesus told some Jews who were angry because he broke the Sabbath with this healing and referred to God as his Father,

— *"What the Son does is always modeled on what the Father does, for the Father loves the Son and* **shows** *him everything that he does himself.... How on earth can you believe while you are for ever* **looking for each other's approval** *and not for the glory that comes from the one God?"*[4]

Later in a conversation with some who followed him, who were believing in him, Jesus said,

— *"The Father has never left me alone for I always do what pleases him."* He told them, *"If you are faithful to what I have said, you are truly my disciples. And you will know the truth and the truth will set you free!.... I am telling you what I have* **seen** *in the presence of my Father, and you are doing what you have* **seen** *in the presence of your father."*

Out of this then arose a statement clear and to the point about the image already in the world and the image coming into the world with the Christ:

— *"Why do you not understand my words? It is because you cannot hear what I am really saying. Your father is the devil, and what you are wanting to do is what your father longs to do. He always was a murderer, and has never dealt with the truth, since the truth will have nothing to do with him. Whenever he tells a lie, he speaks in character, for he is a liar and the father of lies... Believe me when I tell you that if anybody accepts my words, he will_never* **see** *death at all."*[5]

Finally, we come to this story, a story of a man blind from birth who aroused from the disciples the question,

— *"Master, whose sin caused this man's blindness, his own or his parents?"*

What a powerful question when looking at the problem of imaging that is abroad amongst the children of men! We are all blind from birth, unable to **see** how to live, always in the dark and in the shadow of death. Light and life are far from us and we grope about in the darkness like our parents and their parents and their parents. Whose sin caused this?

— *"Not his own nor that of his parents. He was born this way to **show** the power of God at work in him… I am the world's light as long as I am in it."*

Then Jesus healed the man. The story ends with this exchange of Jesus asking,

— *"Do you believe in the Son of Man?" The man replied, "And who is he, sir? Tell me, so that I can believe in him." "You have **seen** him," replied Jesus. "It is the one who is talking to you now." And then he said, "My coming into this world is itself a judgment—those who cannot **see** have their eyes opened and those who think they can **see** become blind."*[6]

All through this time of teaching about himself, the disciples of Jesus kept getting his message mixed up with their own preconceptions and thoughts concerning the kingdom of God and who David's heir, the Messiah, was to be. Jesus finally asked them this question,

— *"Who do people say that the Son of Man is?"*

After several responses, Simon Peter answered,

— *"You? You are Christ, the Son of the living God!"*

The Anointed One! The Messiah! Listen to Jesus' next statement:

— *"Simon, Son of Jonah, you are a fortunate man indeed, for it was not your own nature but my Heavenly Father who has revealed this truth to you. Now I tell you that you are Peter the rock, and it is on this rock that I am going to found my Church and the powers of death will never prevail against it."*[7]

What was revealed? The image of the Father was revealed. God revealed Himself and Peter **saw** it in human flesh. Not the image of a king's authority like the authorities of the nations. Not the image of greed or control or deception or privilege. Not the image like anyone or anything Peter had ever before encountered or known. This was different. What he **saw** in this man and had encountered in the months in his presence was as he had known in no other human being. He recognized the difference that Jesus was not like John the Baptist nor the descriptions of any of the prophets of old. He must be, "He Is!" the Christ! God had revealed Himself!

Now is the fulfillment of what is needed in the portrayal and description of the Christ. All this history of God with Abraham, of the encounter between God and the gift of the law to Moses, of a long history of struggle and failure that finally comes down through a remnant to the hope of creation focused on One Anointed who would be obedient to the image of the eternal One: all this is completed when Peter **saw** it, for once it is truly **seen** in human flesh not as power but humbly and truly as a way of life that can be taught and discipled, then the light of the world will never again go out. It can and will grow like leaven in the lump, like a tiny seed into the greatest of shrubs to shelter life, like light that gives light to all in the house. And Peter, blessed Peter, **saw** it for real! Now Jesus could build the kingdom of God on earth just as it is in eternity. The Christ is come. He is Risen. He will come again. And again. And again. And....

Chapter Recap:

The Christ is the One who reveals God in human flesh, who images the Almighty fully and purely, and who restores to creation the kingdom of God. He is obedient to all that was asked, every holy law that governs relationships in the bond of love. The figure of the Christ was a singular figure of Israel, the nation born of God in the covenant made with Abraham and renewed through history with his children's children. Israel, chosen by God to witness to His life, was to image Him in their daily living under the Commandments of God delivered to the people through Moses. Though they lived in this relationship of covenant to God for centuries, they failed in their calling to witness to His life. They broke His statutes and, like the world they were to redeem, lived the life of the deceiver. Through the faithfulness of God to the covenant made with Israel came a word of hope by which Israel could succeed. A remnant would be faithful to the covenant, and if not the remnant, then one, One, who would be God's servant, Israel, and He would be the obedient life of holiness and obedience who would restore to creation the image of the Creator.

In the fullness of time, Jesus was born, he who was God With Us, the Anointed One called the Messiah, the Christ, and he, by his life lived even through the cruel end of death on a cross, lived as God's servant Israel and fulfilled the witness. The disciples **saw** and proclaimed the truth of his witness to God.

CHAPTER FIVE
INHERITANCE AND THE PROMISE

Finally the Christ is come, the Anointed One, who gives witness to the image of the Creator and reconciles the creation back to its Lord and God. The One who saves the world, God With Us, is come and it is the fullness of time for creation. Jesus is his name. Chapter Four hopefully gave you some sense of the role of the Christ, of the one who lives the image of God faithfully, completely, continually, never succumbing to the choice of showing in the flesh the image of anyone, anything, other than the Creator of all. In so doing, others could see God, and in that vision begin Love's replication themselves. Jesus told his disciples it was possible, he told them that Eternal Life was to be theirs and they could live it. He encouraged them to seek the kingdom's life first, to put its practice ahead of all other desires. He sent them out on their own trial missions to share with others the expression of para-dise and to teach everyone what they themselves had already learned: "...*the kingdom of Heaven has arrived.*"[98] Such a message of hope and life! The scrip-tures tell us they came back rejoicing that, "...*even evil spirits obey.*"[99] But there was much for the Anointed One to do for they also came up against experi-ences in which they could not find their way and the old patterns of living were again the only memories from which to work. A man bringing his son who had a "dumb spirit" found the disciples frustrated by their inability to bring wholeness to the boy. James and John, brothers and sons of Zebedee, could not escape their thoughts of ambition and greed and succumbed to the old habits of trying to manipulate their relationship with Jesus in order to ensure their futures ahead of their friends and fellow disciples:

— "*Teacher we want you to do for us whatever we ask of you... Grant us to sit, one at your right hand and one at your left, in the glory of your kingdom.*"[100]

This, of course, led to the others also losing their hold of Jesus' teaching and image and responding in kind to James and John's witness:

— "*And when the ten heard this, they began to be highly indignant at James and John.*"[101]

On and on the examples go as Jesus used this period to show the grace and power of his own life while all the time using other's lives to illustrate the difference between the kingdom in him, the kingdom in them, and what will be the inheritance that is the promise for all.

The chapter before you is all about the kingdom on earth, the promise of God (our inheritance), and how we obtain it. It is here that the "Way of the Cross" becomes a reality and hopefully an experience that empowers you and sets you free to live as the child of God that you truly are. So let us examine, in sequence, these four themes: the kingdom on earth, the Way of the Cross, the promise of God, and our inheritance.

A. The Kingdom on earth.

Most of us have very little understanding or appreciation for the institution of kingdoms and the authority of kings. The politics of western, democratic institutions have little place for the concept of absolute power and we in the west strive diligently to defend our legacy of personal rights and freedom. But in such places as the British Isles, one can get a sense of the omnipresence of the ruling lord inherent in the monarchial system and how royal ownership pervades every facet of one's life. The land itself reflects it with castles everywhere, with names of cities and counties that reflect ancient boundaries of king's shires, with ruins of abbeys shut down in the reign of Henry VIII simply by his decree. Twenty-first century life is no less influenced by the British royal presence. The currency carries the faces of monarchy or familial seals, Anglican worship prays faithfully for the Queen and royal family, and the very identity of the common person is somehow securely anchored in a system whose tradition and control goes back two thousand years or more. To live here is to be the subject of Her Majesty! One feels it all the time in literal and spiritual things.

In biblical terms, what are we talking about when we talk of a kingdom? Contemporary teaching and evangelism almost exclusively link it to a place. I suspect that has been the Church's claim for some seventeen hundred years, ever since Constantine's conversion began its insidious change upon the fabric of Christian life. For the first generations of converts to The Way, entrance into the community necessitated a wise and reasoned choice, for the life asked of the disciples of the Christ stood most often in identifiable contrast to one's former, personal witness. If one was a Hebrew, newfound liberty in the teachings of Jesus might bring one into conflict with the strict obedience required of Hebrews by the Mosaic law. If one was a Gentile, baptism into Christ might bring one into conflict with the rules and regulations governing secular obedience to the lordship of Caesar. There came those times in the early centuries when it mattered little who one might have been, Jew or Gentile. To be Christian meant to choose to be in conflict, period. Such was the opposition to the lifestyle of the New Covenant community. One chose the Christian life deliberately, seeing it as a way of life by which one might grow in the image of one's Creator, which was made known in human flesh in the Christ. One could *"put on Christ,"*[102] could *"grow up in every way into Christ,"*[103] or, like Paul, simply admit to, and enjoy the miracle of, new birth: *"...it is no longer I who live, but Christ who lives in me."*[104]

But with Constantine came a change in the personal decision-making process for more and more people until the original concept of a new way of living on earth was for the most part lost and a new theology of the next life in heaven or hell arose. Constantine's encouragement of the Christian faith beginning in AD 312 after winning the battle for control of the empire led to Christianity becoming the preferred religion of the Roman world. Thereafter, becoming Christian put one in a social and political light that might be advantageous; the emperor was Christian, you know. It could include one in circles and influence in a time when it was important to be in the right circle; the emperor was Christian, you know. It meant, at the least, not having the obstacle of religion as a roadblock to personal power and privilege; the emperor was Christian. You know! But it also was the beginning of the time when becoming Christian meant only being baptized, just going through the rite of entrance (today it is sometimes referred to as, "getting the child done"). Yes, promises were made to believe in and follow Jesus as risen Savior and Lord but as to actually changing one's lifestyle, one's actual way of living, such no longer was the driving and identifying motive. Being a Christian no longer set one apart in image from the rest of the community. With Constantine's conversion, everyone could safely be Christian, and indeed most were, without imaging the Christ in any shape or fashion. Life in the Roman world still revolved around power and control and authority as it had for generations.

In such a spiritual atmosphere, how must one understand the words of Jesus about the kingdom of his Father and the place called heaven? If the kingdom ushered in by the advent of the Christ was not about a way of living that showed forth the Almighty in perfect image, if it was not about lifestyle, what was it all about? "It (the Christian life) is all about getting to the *next* life! That is what the kingdom of heaven talk is all about and that is where it is, beyond the grave!"

In such a statement that might have been made by anyone from the fourth century on, theology found a convenient, reasonable, and acceptable interpretation to fit the reality of the new experience of how the faith of the Roman empire was unfolding. It fit the needs of the masses of people coming to conversion who wanted a religion but not a new life and it fit the needs of those who increasingly assumed the leadership of the community of faith, the Church, who wanted the same but with authority and control. It would not take too many generations until power and control in the Church would rival, even exceed, the power and control of emperors. How is such power ever given over in such degree to a small number of elite by such a large mass of people? The answer is fear.

Religion Class 101: June, AD 400

Statement for Religion Class Discussion: The kingdom of God and eternal life is another life beyond the grave. God dwells there because of the sin of this world and all who live in it. As a result of our sinful mortality, we cannot be with God and when we die, we will go eternally to hell, which is His punishment for our sin. Hell is a place of eternal suffering. To get to heaven we must repent of past wrong doing, acknowledge that Jesus came to suffer and die in our stead for our sins, and be born again. Then when we die, we can go to heaven to live eternally with God in paradise.

Heaven and hell. Heaven or hell! Contemporary fundamentalism puts it, "Turn or Burn," which is not far in tone from the topic-statement of our imaginary class discussion from the year AD 400. This more and more became the interpretation of Jesus' words recorded in the gospels until the sense of the kingdom on earth and the possibility of being just like the *"firstborn of all creation"*[105] became merely words and unattainable for anyone but Jesus. Why? *Because he was God in human flesh and we are but sinners in human flesh!*

Once again, separation (death) became the teaching of the Covenant people, this time of the New Covenant. Who set the standard for this interpretation? Once again, the hierarchy, this time the leadership of priests and bishops of the Church who by the teaching and sacramental privilege inherited by them from the leadership of the early apostolic community and with the new growing status and power of the post-Constantinian world, effectively exercised control over the rites by which one's eternal destiny was governed. "When all your loved ones are in heaven in the bosom of Abraham at the table set by the living God, where will *you* be?" Fear is a terrible weapon in the hands of spiritual people.

Is there an alternative message to all this and is it a holy, legitimate expression of our heritage? Yes! Moreover, it is the teaching of the scriptures from the beginning and is so clear and simple and holy that it amazes me why the Church universal does not cry out demanding to have its very life set free so that it can help not only its members but the whole world find new life! Jesus was asked by the Pharisees when the kingdom of God was coming and he gave them this reply:

— *"The kingdom of God never comes by watching for it. Men cannot say, 'Look, here it is, or there it is,' for the kingdom of God is inside you."*[106]
INSIDE YOU!

Question: What is needed for a kingdom to exist? The answer: Only the king. Nothing else is required for there to be a kingdom but the person of the king, and nothing can establish a kingdom without this royal person; not land, not armies, not wealth. A kingdom is wherever the king is. Examples exist in the modern world of this very thing. The kingdom of Austria exists in exile because the royal family lives in England and proclaims its existence. The spiritual kingdom of Tibet still exists in exile because the exalted Lama and the process of reincarnation still continues even from afar and presses the Communist leadership of China for return of the land. The ancient precedents in scripture and history are there, as well. Remembering that all that is needed for a kingdom is the presence of the king (or a symbol of him!):

— Joseph in the land of Egypt, when invested with Pharaoh's signet ring, could rule everywhere but in the Pharaoh's family or personal presence. So vested, it was known that pharaoh was present **in** Joseph;

— In medieval England, Edward I built huge castle-fortresses that were never used for war. Their mere presence said that the King was there and in charge.

It is the king and his person that alone establishes the nature and presence of a kingdom. In good humor (most of the time) a man in the sanctity of his home, his apartment, his boat, his whatever, states that he is king of his castle, acknowledging that these are the few and only places that he has much authority or control, and then precious little.

One day, one of the scribes approached Jesus and put a question to him,
— *"What are we to consider the greatest commandment of all?"*
Jesus replied with,
— *"Hear, O Israel: The Lord our God, the Lord is one; and you shall love the Lord your God with all your heart, with all your soul, and with all your mind, and with all your strength. This is the first and great commandment. The second is this; you shall love your neighbor as yourself. No other commandment is greater than these."*

The Christian community calls these familiar words, The Summary of the Law. Hearing Jesus' answer, the scribe made a reply that leads us to something important. Listen.
— *"I am well answered. You are absolutely right when you say that there is one God and no other God exists but him; and to love him with the whole of our hearts, the whole of our intelligence and the whole of our energy, and to love our neighbors as ourselves is infinitely more important than all these burnt offerings and sacrifices."*

Then this, Jesus' answer, when noting the thoughtfulness of the scribe's reply:
— ***"You are not far from the kingdom of God!"***[107]

How could Jesus say that? Was he referring to the scribe's imminent departure to the grave? Obviously not! He was referring to the personal journey, the inner journey, the way-of-life journey that the scribe's reply indicates. Something took root in the scribe in that encounter with Jesus that allowed him to *see* the truth that he wanted and immediately he began to appropriate it as his own. He drew the kingdom of God closer to himself, more within himself. As the thought took hold of beginning to live what he recognized to be the truth, the way and the life would become his, just like in Jesus! All he needed, though he did not yet know it, was the king's presence within to make it happen.

Jesus could personally talk about the kingdom as a reality known and experienced. He could talk of it as always being present. He could talk intimately of the King of the realm and act in His behalf in every situation, for the kingdom was in, indeed *was*, his own flesh and everything he did revealed the activity of the presence of the King. The words that he shared in every conversation were the King's words and the deeds of every moment that people saw were those of the King. From his birth as Mary's firstborn this was so. He was always about his Father's business. When asked to make this intimate relationship with the King more real, more plain, to say it clearly, he told his disciples that their belief in him could rest,

— "*... on the words that I say, or if you can not believe in them, then believe me for the deeds that I do.*"[108]

Wonderfully straightforward. "*The Father and I are one.*"[109] "*The King and his kingdom are in me!*"[110] Jesus was the temple that could be knocked down and rebuilt in three days. He was Paul's "*sanctuary (holy of holies) not made with hands.*"[111] He was the light of life, the living water that eternally flowed, the bread come down from heaven, the resurrection, Ezekiel's good shepherd, the perfect lamb of God. All these things Jesus was and all showed the truth of the kingdom of God as a present, experiential, living reality by which the image of God was seen and a relationship of oneness restored with and in human flesh.

To enter into a relationship with, i.e. to *see*, Jesus, the Christ, was to experience the Kingdom of Heaven, the Kingdom of God, as it was meant to be for all creation.

B. The Way of The Cross

Before we can go any further, we must talk of The Cross. The Christ-life is not understood without it and Jesus said too many things about The Cross and its relationship to the Kingdom and to our lives for it to be avoided. The Cross where Jesus died to "*take away the sins of the whole world.*"[112] what is it really?

From one point of view, that of an observer, the cross was a debilitating instrument of humiliation and cruel death. Used by the Romans with great effectiveness, it had the power to break the will of whole peoples by its selective, public use with a few. Being condemned to die by crucifixion meant being put on public display, subjected to agonizing pain, burdened with the biblical legacy of being cursed of God (in the theology of the Hebrews), enduring the taunts of passers-by, and succumbing to blessed death very slowly.

With Palestine's occupation by the Romans came Roman law and punishment. Israel no longer had legal power over civic justice and, like all people in the province, were entirely subject to the decisions, be they whims or ire or fair justice, of the Roman magistrates. Since Jewish religious law was left to be deliberated by the Jewish Council of priests, pharisees, sadducees and the like, Roman magistrates like Pontius Pilate had neither interest nor time for the myriad statute infractions causally connected by religious expression that affected Hebrew daily life. But crimes, civil or religious, deemed punishable by death were another matter. Only Roman law could exact this decision. When rendered, the death penalty was most often carried out by crucifixion. And selectively used, whole peoples, such as the Hebrews, could easily be controlled.

So it was, that at the end of that period called the fullness of time, Jesus was taken by a band of armed men at the behest of the chief priests and elders of the people and handed over to the Roman magistrate, Pontius Pilate, with a request that he be put to death. His crime? Listen to the scriptures:

— *Again the high priest asked him, "Are you the Christ, the Son of the Blessed?" And Jesus said, 'I AM;'"...*[113]

— *So Jesus came out, wearing the crown of thorns and the purple robe. Pilate said to them, "Behold the man!" When the chief priests and the officers saw him, they cried out, "Crucify him, crucify him!" Pilate said to them, "Take him yourself and crucify him, for I find no crime in him." The Jews answered him, 'We have a Law, and according to that Law—he must die, because he has made himself the Son of God!'"*[114]

Jesus was rejected for being the Christ, the Anointed One! He was told that he broke the law of the Covenant People by being what they all were called to be in their creation and in their Covenant with the Almighty and admitting it. This Christ was condemned to death by sacred law for being the image of the Covenant God. Herein is an interesting thing. Jesus was not condemned for *being* the image of the Holy One, not for living a righteous and sinless life; no, that was not the issue. He was rejected for *saying* he was the image of God, the Christ. Listen again:

— *"Now the chief priests and the whole council sought testimony against Jesus to put him to death; but they found none. For many bore false witness against him, but their witness did not agree. And some stood up and bore false witness against him, saying, 'We heard him say...' Yet not even so did their testimony agree."*[115]

With such words was his passion remembered and his judgment described. Then he was led outside the city of Jerusalem and, on a high hill for all to see, crucified. Innocent of any crime, righteous in the sight of God and many, still spotless and without sin, the lamb was led to the slaughter.

— *"It is better that one man should die than the whole nation perish."*[116]

Do you remember in earlier chapters our making reference to how Jesus went out to a lonely, wild place to wrestle with what was ahead of him and to fast and pray? He had just begun his ministry with meeting John and submitting to his baptism, *"in order to fulfill all righteousness"*[117] (Do you suppose that believers might acknowledge that it is possible that one man should *repent* for the whole nation?). In the long forty days of his fast, the tempter came and Jesus wrestled with options to obedience and how to express his identity and image. When he emerged victorious and sure within himself, we were told, *"The tempter withdrew until a more opportune time."* The apocryphal book called, *The Wisdom of Solomon*, probably written in the latter part of the first century BC, contains a story that witnesses to the reality of the testing and temptation of a more opportune moment:

— *"For they reasoned unsoundly, saying to themselves,... 'Let us lie in wait for the righteous man, because he is inconvenient to us and opposes our actions; he reproaches us for sins against the law, and accuses us of sins against our training. He professes to have knowledge of God, and calls himself a child of the Lord. He becomes to us a reproof of our thoughts; the very **sight** of him is a burden to us, because his manner of life is unlike that of others, and his ways are strange. We are considered by him as something base, and he avoids our ways as unclean; he calls the last end of the righteous happy, and boasts that God is his father. Let us see if his words are true, and let us test what will happen at the end of his life; for if the righteous man is God's child, he will help him, and will deliver him from the hand of his adversaries. Let us test him with insults and torture, so that we might find out how gentle he is, and make trial of his forbearance. Let us condemn him to a shameful death, for, according to what he says, he will be protected.' Thus they reasoned, but they were led astray, for they did not know the secret purposes of God;... for God created us for incorruption, and made us in the image of his own eternity."*[118]

What a powerful story of just what happened in the passion. Jesus, once more, in this drama of betrayal, rejection, denial, cruelty, and intense pain and agony, had to wrestle with himself concerning his commitment to living in the image of God. This is always where the real work must be done, the real battle with sin and temptation: *within*, in the temple of the spirit. For Jesus, the final test started in the garden called Gethsemane after the Passover supper he shared with his disciples. Going apart to pray, Jesus agonized with what now was inevitable:

— *"Father, if you are willing, take this cup away from me—but it is not my will, but yours, that must be done."*[119]

Over and over, the prayer and the conclusion, *". . . not my will, but yours..."* Wrestling, struggling, tempted—but maintaining. Strained, sweat falling like blood to the ground. Tested. Maybe fighting thoughts common to many of us:

"Run! You don't have to be a martyr. No one expects you to have to do this. No one else would, why should you?"

"Join the zealots. This way didn't work. Maybe they are right."

"Lie when they ask you what you said. Who is going to refute it, so many things were said and there were so many people who didn't understand it all anyway."

"Fight, curse them, spit on them, call down angels to kill them!"

"Father-God: DAMN THEM ALL TO HELL!!! I HATE THEM FOR WHAT THEY DO!"

Tempted; one last time; sin's last opportunity.

Jesus stood before them all and uttered not a word. They crucified him by nailing his wrists to the upper plank, his feet to the lower platform, and raised the cross to drop it solidly in the ground. They hung him in the heat of the day in the sight of the people, cursed to a slow death from asphyxiation. Yet, listen closely to his words:

— *"Father, forgive them, they know not what they do...*[120] *It is finished...*[121] *Into your hands I commend my spirit."*[122] And he breathed his last and lowered his head.

— *"If anyone wants to follow in my footsteps, he must give up all right to himself, take up his cross and follow me... The man who tries to save his life will lose it; it is the man who loses his life for my sake and the gospel's who will save it... What good can it do for a man to gain the whole world at the price of his own soul? What can a man offer to buy back his soul once he has lost it?"*[123]

Here is the task for us all. It is the same as Jesus'. It is the struggle to see the kingdom of God within ourselves and create there a temple for the indwelling of our God. Each new day, we are to live our lives as an outward image of the kingdom's inner, personal truth. Thus, we do not wrestle with flesh and blood, but with ourselves. No one takes the glory from us, rather we give it up by personal poor choice. Powers and principalities do not hide behind every bush or tree to attack us; they are the inner options—good, bad, and indifferent—that we muse and mull over as ways to deal with the opportunities or difficulties of each moment. We walk through a world of God's wondrous creation that has been tainted with generations of sin that project other images to and fro and thereby it is a creation filled with risk and chance. It is in meeting the events and personalities of each day of our journey that we are offered opportunities and choices to manifest an image only of our Creator, and the cross is our constant companion in the struggle to maintain that image of the One who loves us so much. Pick the cross up!! It is the hope of the kingdom and the only way to find one's life and to truly come alive. These words I bid you to write on the lintels of your doors, on the mirrors in which you behold your reflection, and on the very flesh of your own heart:

"The way of the cross is the way of life."

C. The Promise of God.

Remember the scribe who asked Jesus about the law? The story ended with Jesus telling him that he was ever so near to the kingdom. I love the truth it proclaims concerning God's desire to see the kingdom within us even as we live in the flesh on the earth. But for the scribe, "near to the kingdom," are like words heard by the dejected son who returns home from playing the homecoming football game that was lost 47 to 48. His well-meaning mother says, "Oh son, don't feel bad. You only lost by one point!" One point or a hundred, the son knows that the game was still lost. "Near to the kingdom" is still outside the kingdom. The power of that story from scripture is the movement in the heart of the scribe that allowed him to begin to see the Spirit's work.

Now it is important for us to understand clearly what makes it possible for us to not only see the image of God in Jesus and proclaim him the Christ but to claim the same reality in ourselves and live as the sons and daughters of our Creator, showing clearly His image. It all has to do with, "*the promise of the Father.*"[124]

A quick review might here be helpful. The name, Jesus, means, "*Yahweh (God) saves.*" The child in Mary's womb was to be called Emmanuel, which means, "*God with us.*" The Christ, the Anointed One, was Ezekiel's shepherd-Messiah, God who would come clothed in humanity's flesh to be what Israel was failing to be. The person of the Christ is the Creator-Spirit (GOD) incarnate, that is, in human flesh. The firstborn of all humanity's family is Jesus Christ in whom for the first time we understand the universal, eternal reality of the work of atonement, God and man becoming at-one as it was and is meant to be.

— Philip said to him, "*Show us the Father, Lord, and we shall be satisfied.*" Jesus said to him, "*... He who has seen me has seen the Father...Do you not believe that I am in the Father and the Father is in me?*"[125]

— It was the feast of the Dedication at Jerusalem. The Jews said to him, "*How long will you keep us in suspense? If you are the Christ, tell us plainly.*" *Jesus answered them, "...I and the Father are One.*"[126]

— "*I am not praying only for these men but for all those who will believe in me through their message, that they all may be one...I have given them the honor that you gave me, that they may be one, as we are one—I in them and you in me, that they may grow complete into one, so that the world may realize that you sent me and have loved them as you loved me.... I want them to see that glory which you have made mine—for you loved me before the world began.... I have made your self known to them and I will continue to do so that the love which you have had for me may be in their hearts—and that I may be there also.*"[127]

The Trinity is a theological mystery that has caused all sorts of pain for Christians through the centuries as the Church wrestled to define and protect the faith once delivered to the Apostles. In an effort to ensure both the humanity and the divinity of Jesus, theology finally settled on an explanation that the one true God who alone existed without body, parts, or passion before all things came to be was indeed three persons, of one substance, power, and eternity: The Father, the Son, and the Holy Spirit. Three yet one; one God of three persons. Three in one and one in three. Trinity.

I believe it, the Trinity. I believe that the Son and the Father and the Spirit always existed and always will and that they are indeed one God, one Lord, one Spirit. I, however, am more simplistic in trying to make sense of things (that is why I'm writing this, so that it does not take you forty years or more to try to catch the truth of Love) and therefore have come to understand the Trinity in this way:

— The one and only God is Spirit, just as Jesus told the woman at the well. This God is neither here or there but is to be worshiped in spirit and in truth everywhere. All that exists in creation is the result of the Creator's energy, which is Love, God's nature: God is Love. When creation failed to reflect that nature, the concluding act of redemptive salvation was God putting on human flesh in the incarnation of Jesus, born to the woman, Mary, upon whom the **Spirit** of God came so that the child would be **Son** of God, or said conversely, God would be his **Father**. It also helps me when I look at this incarnation and the annunciation of Mary from a Semitic point of view. The man, the father, was the life-giver; his role in the act of conception was to place the new life into the womb. The woman's role was to carry or bear that life safely as that life grew to term and birth; she had no part in the creation of that life, she only carried it. Therefore, for Mary, the life-giver for the son she carried was God; **Father**. So, too, for Jesus, and he was quick to say so: "*Did you not know that I must be in my Father's house?*"[128] So, too, for all of us as we learn to pray, "*Our Father who art in heaven....*" But we see specifically (and only) that which God, who is **Spirit**, intended by His incarnation. We see Jesus, who though he was in the form of God... took the form of a servant, born in the likeness of men. In that humanity, he was and is the image of the invisible God, the firstborn of all creation—**Son**. Son of God and Son of Man. Finally, back and around we come with Mary and Jesus and the woman at the well and most truly all humanity: who is this unseen God who visits us as "promise" and "counselor," this unseen Spirit? This **Spirit**! This Spirit is the **Father**. This Spirit is the **Son**. These three, they are One. Trinity.

WHEW!

Now we can get on. The public ministry of Jesus the Christ that is recorded in the four Gospels of the New Testament lasted maybe three years at the most. As it came near to an end, Jesus began to prepare his disciples for the reality that he would be taken from them by arrest and be put to death by crucifixion. Such news is never easily received and the disciples wanted him to deny its reality and stay with them. It could not and would not be so. Jesus did, however, tell them that his going was not only reality but was also in redemption's plan and a necessary and good thing for them. His going would result in the things that he was doing, which is to say the image that he was showing, also occurring in them:

— "*I assure you that the one who believes in me will do the same things that I have done, yes, and will do even greater things than these... If you really love me, you will keep the commandments I have given you and I shall ask the Father to give you someone else... the Spirit of truth... to be with you... to be in your hearts. I am not going to leave you alone in the world—I am coming to you.*[129]

Do you hear and see it? The eternal Spirit in Jesus that is the eternal Father in heaven who finally sees His image perfectly and beautifully exhibited in this beloved Son will now, through the Son's offering in death on the cross, come to be the image with and in us all. *"I (God) am coming to you. I will not leave you alone in the world."* Jesus said this! *"When that day comes, you will realize that I am in my Father, that you are in me, and I am in you."*[130]

It is a promise. It is the full and only promise of the Christian faith. It is the promise that restores things to the way they were created to be.

On that Passover week some two thousand years ago, Jesus was led out of Jerusalem bound to the upper beam of a cross and led to the hill called Golgotha where he was crucified and died. Three days later, the tomb in which he had been laid was found empty, the heavy stone no longer in front of the door. Immediately, several people who knew and loved him began to see him and returned to tell others, "Jesus is alive! He has been raised from the dead and has appeared to us! We have seen him and have talked with him!" The physician, Luke, a believer and acquaintance of both Peter and Paul, wrote of these appearances in both his Gospel and in the book called the Acts of the Apostles. In <u>Acts</u>, he records this:

— *"For after his suffering he showed himself alive to them in many convincing ways and appeared to them repeatedly over a period of forty days talking with them about the affairs of the kingdom of God. On one occasion, while he was eating a meal with them, he emphasized that they were not to leave Jerusalem, but to wait for the Father's promise."*

— *'You have already heard me speak about this,' he said, 'for John used to baptize with water, but before many days are passed you will be baptized with the Holy Spirit.'*[131]

The Father's promise is the Spirit. The promise of God to us is God, Himself. God comes to us, to be with us and dwell in us. God in us. Emmanuel. We are to be just like Jesus. The way that it happens is the indwelling of God, the Spirit. We are all made again, finally, the children of God in whom His image is to be seen. It is the promise, the WORD of the Lord. And did it happen as he said it would?

— *"And when the actual day of Pentecost came they were all assembled together... Suddenly... a sound... like the rush of a violent wind... tongues like flames... above the head of each... they were all filled with the Holy Spirit... to proclaim his message... Then Peter addressed them (Jews of deep faith from every nation of the world)... this is something which was predicted by the prophet Joel, "And it shall be in the last days, saith God, I will pour forth of my Spirit upon all flesh..."*[132]

Jesus, God saves, told his disciples that he would come again to them.

God, the creating Spirit of Love, indeed did come to them, just as He promised—as He promised with Joel, as He promised with the Baptist, as He promised with Jesus. He came, and not only to the waiting disciples and those gathered together that feast-day of Pentecost, but to all flesh. He came to them, He came to me, He came to you. He (God) came to all who were, who are, and who ever will be. It is the Word of the Lord! Peter, Joel, John, and Jesus agree!

So many things are taught about gifts and fruits and what we will receive when we get to heaven. I hope that you have begun to see something much more wondrous and honest. We, the children of grace, who follow in the lineage of the firstborn—Jew and Gentile, slave and free, male and female, good and bad, believer and unbeliever—we have received everything that there is to receive and everything that is worth receiving: we have received the living God! We are, *in our flesh*, the inheritors of eternal life.

D. The Inheritance

We are often told that there are two topics of discussion never to get caught up in: politics and religion. Friendships can be lost and new enemies made. There is great truth to this! But being a priest in the Church, it has been difficult for me not to venture opinions concerning religion for that is what I am called to be about in my ordination. I am to preach and teach the scriptures and help people find a living relationship with our Creator. Reading and applying the scriptures to the complexities of life necessarily demands an opinion on what the authors of sacred stories and memory meant. Trying to live my own example of the image of God says to those who watch me that I have an opinion, and it has caused me to act and/or speak in a certain way. Even the first disciples stated this. Peter and John, when charged not to speak or teach at all in the name of Jesus, replied,

— *"Whether it is right in the eyes of God for us to listen to what you say rather than to what he says, you must decide; for we cannot help speaking about what we have actually seen and heard!"*[33]

To talk about the inheritance is to venture into the territory comprised mainly of opinions. By definition, inheritance usually necessitates the death of the owner of that which is to be inherited. Wills are not read and/or probated until the author of the document has died. Then the transfer of property is executed and one is said to be an inheritor of the estate.

How interesting. Why is it, do you suppose, that most Christians only speak in terms of what they shall inherit upon their own death rather than the death of the One who owns what they hope to gain? Could it be that we have the message wrong? We'll get to this shortly. The common man's theology of the Church for the past seventeen hundred years has fixated almost exclusively on seeking to inherit heaven and the riches thereof and have used such visions (dare I say, opinions?) as the Revelation of John with which to define what heaven and its inheritance should be. It is a place through and beyond the clouds of immense beauty and wealth, of jewels and gold, where the physical needs of shelter and food are provided, and where there is only everlasting bliss and pleasure and plenty for those who get there. It is also a place where the problems of non-believers will neither occur or afflict *us*, the believers, because *they* shall be cast into outer darkness where there will be weeping and gnashing of teeth. That is a very modest summary of what is believed! When shall all this be mine, in that I am a believer? As soon as I pass through the gate of death and the grave!

Wrong! Two things must be remembered and considered. They are:

— Biblically (see chapter 2), death does not refer to the cessation of bodily activity and our going to the grave. It refers to separation from our creator, so that what others see in our sin does not reflect upon the true holiness of the living God. The image seen in us in death (separation) is the image not of God but of an impostor, a liar. Separation from the only God is death.

— Inheritance comes at the physical death of the one who owns what is willed, not at the physical death of the one who inherits. It is not our going to the grave that is the issue but rather the going to the grave of the one who has what we desire and need to inherit. For Christians, we are talking then of Jesus and his passion.

Now, consider these two things as we talk of that event called the passion:

— When did Jesus die in a biblical sense, that is, when was he separated from God for you and me and *"for the sins of the whole world?"* Remember: the story of the scriptures and the truth of the witness that Jesus made that finally led a few to recognize him as the Christ was that he was never separate from God. Jesus always reflected the image of the eternal One from beginning to end. He and his Father were one always! The story of all four Gospels is that Jesus was at every moment of his life one with his heavenly Father, always saying and doing only that which was the perfect image of the words and actions of the Creator. The witness of the first century Church agrees with that at every juncture, both from its Hebrew and its Gentile perspectives. Jesus was never separate from God in the witness of his flesh! He was always alive! Only one instance and one moment records a separation from his God and Father: "Eli, Eli lama sabachthani?" (*"My God, my God, why did you forsake me?"*)[134] Here is the awful, eternal, experience of separation, of the pain and fear of death's sting. Jesus, while still struggling to survive and complete what is the purpose of the sacrificial lamb in the rite of the atonement, accepts death for all of God's fallen creation. And then, one more great cry: *"It is finished."*[135]

— Jesus yielded up his spirit, his body stopped its functioning, and his flesh died. What the disciples knew and touched, the one who they saw and listened to, he who broke the bread and washed their feet, his flesh was broken completely and he now must be taken from the tree and placed in the grave. He was no more. What did the disciples and those who knew and loved Jesus have left? What was their legacy from him? This is the question once the great stone was rolled across the entrance of the tomb, and all of the chosen ones sensed it and came up desperately short-handed. They had nothing! Their hopes, their plans, their work of these many past months: all gone. Even their memory of what he had told them failed. They had no inheritance at all with which to carry on or prosper. At his burial, nothing was theirs; nothing at all. Various stories reflect the state of mind of the disciples. One says that two disciples left for home back in Emmaus, full of despair. Another talks of ten of the remaining disciples hiding in a locked, closed room for fear that they, too, might be persecuted like Jesus. Yet another speaks of Peter and several others returning to what they were familiar with: fishing. The point is, having nothing left with which to carry on, they prepare to get on with life in the ways of their former image. There was no inheritance to be proffered them once Jesus was gone. Seemingly...

"Why do you look for the living among the dead? He is not here..."[136] Such was the message to Mary of Magdala to whom Jesus appeared first. She went and reported this to his sorrowing and weeping followers. They heard her say that he was alive and that she had *seen* him, but they did not believe it. But, in the mystery of the resurrection, God and man were one again and the appearances of such began: to those who, hearing Mary's story, ran to the tomb to look for themselves; then to the ten in the locked room; then to the two on their way to Emmaus; then to Thomas with the rest of the brethren. Then Luke describes forty days of Jesus' presence with them and the message concerning "the promise of the Father" which would be their inheritance: the Holy Spirit. Later, Paul would write of this inheritance and gift as a great mystery *"hidden for the ages but now revealed"* and describe it as a means by which we *"who died to the elemental spirits of the universe"* now live. He called this new life, *"Christ in us, the hope of glory"*![137]

How might we honestly and realistically talk of this inheritance, free of the bonds of the words inherited and translated and interpreted for generations, free to find something real and life-giving for ourselves? Try it this way:

— I have claimed the inheritance stemming from Jesus' death for my sins as a new life reconciled to his Father and mine. The Almighty One, God my Creator, has now given me the inheritance that comes from His own atoning sacrifice and that inheritance is Himself. He who is Eternal Spirit has come to reveal His presence to my soul and taken up residence in my flesh. No longer separated from Him because of my sins (though they are real and many, they have been covered with the blood of Jesus) nor living in fear of judgment (my guilty verdict has already been decreed and I was crucified with Christ), I am free to live, truly and consciously. I am one with the Eternal One: God and I are one. I have my inheritance: it is that Life who alone is Eternal.

— My inheritance of the Spirit of God, reckoned unto me through the death of the righteous lamb of God, is the proof-positive that death no longer has any dominion over, any power to touch, me again. I have died and I have been raised to life with the Christ, already! Having died with him to sin once, I shall never die again. There no longer is any fear of what is nor of what is yet to be; God and I are now, and will eternally be, one. When the days of my flesh, which are finite and numbered, come to an end, God, my Father, and I will continue just as Jesus has made us to be: reconciled and one! Alive! With the Christ, the life I now live is the resurrected life and, together with the risen Lord, I share eternity already with the One who is Eternal Life! Such is my inheritance!

— I am the son of God. So also are you the son/daughter of God. You and I are not Jesus, nor are we the Christ. But we are the sons and daughters of the living God! All of us! There is no one left out of that inheritance. Let me say this again so that you read it with all the power that it is meant to have: the sin and death of the whole world has been covered and therefore removed by the atoning sacrifice of Jesus, and all of the cosmos is reconciled, made one with, our Creator and Father Eternal! By one sacrifice, all who were once consigned to disobedience and death have had mercy reckoned to them.[138] *"For as in Adam all die, so also in Christ shall all be made alive."*[139] It is the way by which *"God may be everything to every one."*[140] We are all born anew as the sons and daughters of God, now! I am God's son, His child, in whom His image can be seen and His kingdom experienced. We are not strangers to His covenant of grace nor hired servants who will not share His glory. We are not rejects, castoffs, or aliens to the household of His redeeming Love. We have a home, we have a table to be nourished from, we have a family who will give life to our journey. We will never be alone! We belong, we are chosen. We are accepted as precious in His sight not on the basis of any action (good or bad) on our part but purely on the basis of the obedience to Love of our elder Brother, God's firstborn: Jesus. He and he alone has opened the gates of eternal life, torn down the walls of destruction and bondage, and thrown away the keys that kept us separate from God and each other. God is my Father and I am His son. Now, and for all eternity.

AND YOU ALSO ARE HIS BELOVED SON OR DAUGHTER!

CHAPTER RECAP:

The promise of God to His creation is God. Himself. Period. When we have Him, we have all things and lack nothing, either in this life or the life to come. He comes to be one with us, in us. Therefore, the kingdom of God is also in us, just as Jesus said.

This all is ours by inheritance, and the promise of that inheritance in the

Covenant (Will) is His Spirit which came to all humanity in fulfillment of Joel's prophecy and witnessed to by Peter and the first Church community. By His Spirit, the mystery hidden for all ages waiting to be revealed in the passion of Jesus and his resurrection was made known and that mystery is Christ is us, the hope of our glory. Therefore, we shall never have to live in the shadow or fear of death (separation) again. We have all died with Jesus, the Christ, and we have all likewise been raised with him to be in the presence of the Father.

Jesus, who has gone before us, dwells in eternity to make continued intercession in our behalf out of the love with which he bore our sins on the tree. We who yet live in the flesh live as the sons and daughters of God, not as strangers or as aliens to the kingdom of His grace. We are His children, the sheep of His pasture, and His family forever. All this is true because of the atoning life and sacrifice of Jesus at Calvary.

Chapter Six
Kingdom Life

We have come a long way so far on this journey together and I hope have found some markers that make the spiritual quest easier and more relevant. Further, I pray that what you have seen and read has blessed you with a sense of the freedom that is ours as we humbly and prayerfully express our soul's inheritance. This life of being the sons and daughters of the Most High is not something overlaid with a covering of fear or guilt nor is it a journey under the threat of judgment and punishment. Rather, it is the expression in word and deed of a great Love by which the whole creation has been renewed with the embrace and presence of its Creator. It is accompanied by the encouragement to witness to the image of the Spirit with which we have been re-created and in that Spirit to help others call forth in themselves that same wondrous image.

Yet as we look around at the reality of the world to which we have been born, our senses tell us that the message proclaimed in scripture and in this short book must be a failure, that the great amount of suffering and hatred that face us on every side bear testimony to the victory of an anti-Christ that seeks to create his own image even as we step forth on our day's journey. If the kingdom of our God is real, and if the call to image the Creating Spirit that was and is and is to be has merit, then how does it happen and what is the specific work to which we who accept the message are enjoined? That is the context of this chapter. I call it the Kingdom Life, the work of Love.

A. Love Is The Key!

If ever there was an overworked word and/or idea in the English tongue, it is "love." It is the substance of our literature and the heartbeat of our music. Fantasies are born of it to carry our dreams in the night and the day-dreams with which we fill our wildest hopes. Love and sex are intricately entwined, so much so as to make the words virtually synonymous for many: "Let's make love." We love to eat, love the Chicago Bulls, love long walks on the beach on a warm, misty morning, and love the raccoons that come to the edge of the brook that courses by our home. Finally, having used the word to convey so many feelings and thoughts, we run the risk that afflicts most all of us—we no longer say what we mean or mean what we say: "I love pot-roast and potatoes; my dog, Spot; vacations to Disneyland; having my back rubbed; and keeping my Harley in top running order. Oh. I love you, too, dear; please pass the pot-roast, will you?" We fall in love and just as quickly fall out of love. It is mind-boggling!

Yet, Love is the key. It is the foundational experience of all that gives life to the world, creating order out of the chaos that is always but a breath away. Maybe that is the sense—foundational life of the world—with which we might try to define what Love is and what its life and power is in us. To do so, I want you to change an image that is probably fundamental to our think-ing, having existed since our earliest memories. It is the image of God.

Most of us inherit an idea of God that is anthropomorphic in nature. We think of God in human terms and in human form. It has been easy for us to have this image. The limitations of human language encourage it and the process by which we describe and share experiences and memories uses men-tal pictures that our minds can only receive and process in the framework of existing patterns, and those patterns are finite and anthropomorphic, i.e. in human context. Hence, God is a person like us with shape and a body, size, and color. Our stories come to us so as to identify God as a man; we call *Him* Father and conceptualize *Him* as an older, bearded, robed figure sitting on a throne in a scene of misty, mystic glory from which *He* rules over and takes account of all creation. Such a scene is easy for us in that the language of scripture's more apocalyptic writings speak in such terms. Moreover, we have seen pictures since our childhood of the biblical Jesus, a Semitic person in the garb of first century mid-eastern culture, and since Jesus is God, then God must look like Jesus. To see one is to know the other, and the Spirit-Father who is the other therefore must have all the physical characteristics of the finite Son.

Though it is natural and very easy to think in this way, it nonetheless is not an accurate or ultimately helpful image. More so, it is detrimental and binding upon our freedom to be the children of God, that which is our inher-itance. If God is an anthropomorphic being, what color is He: white, yellow, black, red? Is He really male or could *He* be, in truth, *She* (Our Mother who art in heaven...)? Is God's shape fat or thin? Does God have cerebral palsy or spina bifida? Does the Creator use glasses to read or dentures to eat? All of us need a God who understands the particular journey and experience life has dealt to us and therefore we see God according to the factors that reflect our own moments. Such factors cause great problems for us in that our defini-tions from the limitations of language and our own moments conflict with the language and the experiences of our neighbors. For instance, what do you suppose the image of God as Father conveys to a child who has been brutalized verbally and physically by his or her birth-father? Can such a child, will such a child, hear the proclamation, "Your heavenly Father loves you," and accept it? You know the answer! Or, if the Lord of our stained-glass windows is white and we are the black great-grandchildren of those brought in chains as bond-slaves to work the fields of white masters, and if our own current living still labors under the burden of prejudices and poverty inherited from that experience, will we hear and live out the bidding of the Lord to love and forgive those who hate you, still turning the other cheek?

Jesus said to the woman at the well:

— *"... the time is coming when worshiping the Father will not be a matter of 'on this hillside' or 'in Jerusalem'. Nowadays you are worshiping with your eyes shut... the time is coming, yes, and has already come, when true worshipers will worship the Father in spirit and in reality. Indeed, the Father looks for people to worship him like that. God is Spirit, and those who worship him can only worship in spirit and in reality."*[141]

The author of the Gospel of John writes that, *"No one has ever seen God...,"* and also, *"Not that anyone has ever seen the Father..."*[142] God is spirit; God is THE Spirit! Unseen, without form, neither finite or with substance, God is pure spirit. BUT, God *is!* God exists! From before time unto forever, GOD.

Therefore, it behooves us to try to put forth another image of God and proclaim a clearer definition that will give all of us revelation, that will give to every human being in every generation a picture that is true to the witness of the Creator whose work in the beginning was intended as a self-revelation.

In chapter one, I shared the concept that being created in the image of God had to do with relationships. God's nature was seen in relationships and after disobedience came, time waited for the advent of the man Jesus in order for relationships to show the true nature of God. Jesus' disciples, being the recipients of his love in relationships that were worked out in daily, experiential examples common to all our humanity, conveyed this experience as the Good News to those who would listen. They told story after story of Jesus' relationships with people he met in everyday, common experiences, stories that revealed the Spirit who creates and re-creates. He healed the sick, he calmed the fearful, he welcomed the children. He comforted the grieving, protected those in flight, fed the hungry. He brought freedom to the damned, forgave those who were alienated, and reconciled the conflicted. Because he did all this by entering into relationship with each that he met rather than remaining uninvolved from afar, the disciples saw something brand new, something they themselves neither had, nor had witnessed in others. They saw Love. For the first time. The author of the pastoral letters attributed to John wrote the following:

— *"To us, the greatest demonstration of God's love for us has been his sending his only Son into the world to give us life through him. We see real love, not in the fact that we loved God, but that he loved us and sent his Son to make personal atonement for our sins. If God loved us as much as that, surely we, in our turn, should love each other.*"[143]

This passage fits Jesus' own words to his brethren on the last evening together for the Passover meal,

— *"Now I am giving you a new command—love one another. Just as I have loved you, so must you love one another.*"[144]

When he had earlier washed their feet, he told them,

— *"I have given you this as an example so that you might do as I have done.*"[145]

And when he broke the bread in the meal and blessed the cup after, he told them,

— *"Do this in remembrance of me.*"[146]

Of this sacramental meal, Paul taught that,

— *"...this can only mean that whenever you eat this bread or drink of this cup, you are proclaiming that the Lord has died for you, and you will do that until he comes again.*"[147]

Jesus prayed earnestly that the twelve, and indeed all of us, would get the message right about his life:

— *"Father of goodness and truth, the world has not known you, but I have known you and these men know that you sent me. I have made your self known to them and I will continue to do so that the love which you have had for me may be in their hearts—and that I may be there also.*"[148]

Relationships. Relationships of love. God seen in our relationships. God seen in our relationships of love. This is the way of God and it is how God reveals his own nature and being. It leads the Church and an author of scripture to boldly proclaim, *"God is love."*[149] I hope that you hear it and feel it for it is in getting to this understanding which enables us to make a change in our imagery of God away from an anthropomorphic understanding to the spiritual truth of Love being the creating energy, the Eternal Life, the redeeming, reconciling Spirit that orders the universe. God is Love, pure and holy.

However, in so doing, it becomes absolutely vital that we maintain a holy witness to this proclamation that denies any opportunity for the deceiver to steal the revelation under the guise that proclaims, "Love is God." There are rules in the discipline of symbolic logic that help make sense of the difference so as to prevent this kind of misinterpretation, but most of us do not apply that mode of reasoning. A simple example may help to illustrate my caution before we go on. One can say truthfully, "All blood is red." One cannot, however, truthfully reverse it: "Everything red is blood." There are red flowers, red cars, red dresses, and so on. We can proclaim, "God is Love" and deny the liar the ability to say, "love is God." We must do so in order to prevent a hedonistic world still struggling with the shadow of disobedience from making the sexual love called Eros, God, or the consuming lust for material possessions and things, God. They may be gods in the sense that Paul identified them as one of *"the many lords and gods"* abroad in this world.[150] Indeed, they are the foundational powers imaged in the lives of many of us. But, they are not *the* God *"which comes down from heaven, and gives life to the world."*[151]

God is Love. Love is made known in relationships. Do you remember that in an earlier chapter we referred to the Law that Moses received for the people on the mountain called Sinai? We used it to make the point that the image of God (now also referred to as the image of Love) could be seen in the way that people treated each other: do not kill each other, do not steal from each other, do not commit adultery against each other, and so forth. That way of relating still expresses life for the recipients of the New Covenant and the inheritors of the witness of Jesus. To live faithfully and honestly with one another in these commandments does make God known, does reveal Love's image. Listen to this from the apostle, Paul, as he tries to teach the life of Christ to the New Covenant flock in Rome:

— *"Keep out of debt altogether, except the perpetual debt of love which we owe one another. The person who loves his neighbor has obeyed the whole Law in regard to the neighbor. For the commandments, 'Thou shall not commit adultery', 'Thou shall not kill', 'Thou shall not steal', 'Thou shall not covet', and all other commandments are summed up in this one saying: 'Thou shall love thy neighbor as thyself.' Love hurts nobody: therefore love is the answer to the Law's commands."*[152]

Jesus' sayings called "The Sermon on the Mount," Matthew 5-7, are all about Love's witness. There he links this work of grace directly and precisely to our Heavenly Father:

— *"For if you love only those who love you, what credit is that to you? Even tax-collectors do that! And if you exchange greetings only with your own circle, are you doing anything exceptional? Even the pagans do as much. No, you are to be perfect, like your Heavenly Father."*[153]

And this, one last reference to Love to help us acknowledge the consistent volume of scripture that points to this truth of the image and the nature of God. Paul expands our understanding of the Creator as he teaches about the Spirit of the Eternal:

— *"God works through different people in different ways, but it is the same God who achieves his purposes through them all. Each person is given his gift by the Spirit that he may use it for the common good... You should set your hearts on the best spiritual gifts, but I will show you a way which surpasses them all... In this life there are three great lasting qualities—faith, hope, and love... the greatest of them is love... Love knows no limits to its endurance, no end to its trust, no fading of its hope; it can outlast anything. It is, in fact the one thing that still stands when all else has fallen... follow, then, the way of love."*[154]

I want you to hear once more and know deep within your soul this clear proclamation before we pass to the next idea:

72

GOD IS LOVE

The Creator-power of the cosmos is Love. The Eternal Life that was and is and ever shall be is Love. The Energy of life and the Source of the light that enlightens every creature is Love. The great "I Am Who I Am" is Love.

B. The Life of *The Give-away.*

Kingdom life (and the way of Love) is all wrapped up in *The Give-away.* For years I have tried to find a word or words that somehow would help to make Love known in a way that fits most every instance and/or experience. I have also wanted something with which to make the life called *The Way of the Cross* meaningful to twentieth-century pilgrims. *The Give-away,* for me, fits as well as anything that I have found.

How can believers, disciples of the Christ, live life so as to image the Eternal One? In the early '90s, my wife and I were blessed to participate in a medical mission to Guatemala. There were about forty-five participants on the mission and our base camp was located in a church compound in the northeast corner of the country. The team was comprised of medical personnel, adult support people, and a small group of senior-high youth who, with advisors, were along to do some construction and repair projects at a local church. I went as chaplain.

Several of the youth took portable CD players along and were very visible with them as they came and went through the local areas. The day soon came when, upon returning in the evening from the work project, it was found that the CD players were gone, stolen. Great anger and judgment followed against those who would do such a thing, accompanied by the inevitable discouragement and disillusionment with the trip, the country, and life in general.

In the evening, gathering for prayer and re-commitment of our lives to our Lord before taking our rest, I quietly suggested that those who had lost items of value to theft that day now make the personal choice to "Give the lost objects away. Make them a gift to the person/persons who now possessed them, for nobody can take from you that which you choose to give away as a gift. It is the only way to heal your heart and dispel the spirit of anger and judgment. Make the objects you valued so much a gift of your love."

Over the thirty-three plus years of my parish ministry, I did many hundreds of weddings, along with the pre-requisite counseling that prepares couples for their special day. The required pre-marital counseling was an important function in my ministry, a function that I took very seriously. Over the years, I fashioned a message that, for me, dealt with the foundational commitment demanded of Christian marriage. I shared it in five sessions in the hope that couples would catch the vision of the work and the joy ahead of them. It is a message of love, the God-love, called Agape. I used the wonderful insights of C. S. Lewis from *The Four Loves* as a basis for the first session and tried to illustrate the differences between the loves translated from the Greek as parental love, friendship love, sexual love, and the God-love. The first three have a common characteristic: they are self-seeking; they arise naturally in us to satisfy our own needs. The God-love alone exists to give itself away; it is self-giving. The first three we all have as a part of our humanity in our birth. The God-love we have as a gift from the Giver that comes to us supernaturally. The first three have a tendency, left to their own energy, to turn from love to pain and division since self-gratification always takes life from others to try to satiate its own desire. The God-love alone remains always as love for it takes nothing from, but rather gives life to, the beloved. Therefore, it is the life of and for the marriage, and the one thing capable of taming and giving real meaning to that which is right and healthy and of value in the other three loves.

The God-love is biblically expressed best in, *"For God so loved the world that he gave..."*[155] you know the rest. Love as the Give-away means 100 percent-zero percent: *"I give my life and love to you 100%; nothing is owed for it in return."* This love is neither a contract nor a bargain. It does not reflect the idea of, "I will if..." The beloved does not have to earn love nor be worthy of it. It is absolutely free, a gift and an offering from the lover to the beloved. It is unconditional in its application and intent. It is the full meaning of, ". . . for better or worse, for richer or poorer, in sickness and in health, to love and to cherish until we are parted by death. This is my solemn vow."[156]

"I GIVE ME TO YOU TO HELP YOU FIND LIFE IN YOU THAT IS THE FULLEST YOU AND LOVE CAN MAKE IT!"

It—this expression of God, the Spirit's full image of Love—is often called The Way of the Cross. We have mentioned this in earlier chapters. The Way of the Cross for us is our coming to grips with Jesus' statements about how to follow him, how to be his disciples:

— *"If you would be my disciple, then you must take up your own cross... if you wish to find your life you must lose it for my sake... those who lose their own lives for me find their lives..."*[157]

The early description of the believing community was called "The Way."[158] I believe it to be a good description, a reflection, of the give-away in the early discipled community for we are told that they,

— *"...shared everything in common... they sold their possessions and goods and divided the proceeds among the fellowship according to individual need... not one of them claimed any of his possessions as his own but everything was common property. The apostles continued to give their witness to the resurrection of the Lord Jesus with great force, and a wonderful spirit of generosity pervaded the whole fellowship. Indeed, there was not a single person in need among them... they would distribute to each one according to his need."*[159]

74

Many today say it is not possible to live this way, that it is not what faith in the witness of Christ asks. Listen some more:

— *"If one hits your right cheek, turn the other one to him as well. If someone wants to sue you for your coat, let him have it and your overcoat as well. If anybody forces you to go a mile with him, do more—go two miles with him. Give to the man who asks anything from you, and don't turn away from the one who wants to borrow."*[160]

What and how much are we willing to give away for the sake of having a relationship with another or others? This is the fundamental question that underlies every human journey! Married life, family life, community life, work life, social life; all depend on how much each of us is willing to sacrifice for the sake of those who share the experience with us. No human relationship can long exist nor any community survive if the individual members thereof do not continuously give of themselves and their possessions for the sake of the common good. Life is found through giving; death results from taking. Every marriage thrives on the spirit of, "What can I do for you this day?" and every child grows strong and sure through the witness of parents whose interest and care is measured by the sacrifice of time, presence, energy, and consistent attitude.

How many of the communities of contemporary culture reel under the emotional, social and financial burdens resulting from adults who no longer sacrifice personally for the sake of spouse or child? Finding it easier to quit and leave rather than lay aside one's wants and desires, half (and in some places, more) of today's marriages crumble, leaving behind those with whom we made covenant commitments to wither under the image of a lost self-worth. Anger, fear, vengefulness come as new companions for the heart. The search for comfort and release from pain find too-willing offerings from addictive and destructive habits. We are naive if we presume that our personal decisions to quit and abandon others do not affect the communities in which we exist and indeed the strength and life of the whole of creation. Do we not hear clearly that

— *"...God has harmonized the whole body... that the body should work together as a whole with all the members in sympathetic relationship with one another. So it happens that if one member suffers all the other members suffer with it, and if one member is honored all the members share a common joy."*[161]

As Paul applies this analogy to the Church, so also is it true for all of the Almighty's creation! We are in this journey, all of it and with everything, together, either to have life in all its abundance or to exist in the throes of death. Schools, churches, neighborhoods, businesses—none can survive when sacrifice is removed from the scene.

The Way of the Cross is a way of life, a chosen journey by which one relates to the encounters and experiences of daily living. It is one of many ways by which human beings can travel from birth to the grave. You and I know these ways for we encounter them every day, and more than likely we have tried and rejected many of them ourselves.

There are addictive ways: to power, sex, food, drugs, work, and more. There are ways of hate and prejudice, dominance and control, and violent, unpredictable anger. There are ways of exploitation, ways of waste and destruction, ways of fear and timidity. It might be safe to say that there are as many ways of life as there are people, for each of us struggles with powers and principalities within that seek to keep us in bondage, unable to find the potential for which our names were first spoken by the Creator who called us into existence.

The way to freedom from these lesser gods is always the same: a conscious choice to replicate, or image, the life of the first One who created us, who is the true Father of our being. Then we can enter upon the journey of self-giving. Then we can embrace the power of the Give-away. Then we can find the Way of the Cross to be the way of life. We shall know the truth inherent in it, that it is in giving life that we find life, in loving that we know Love. And let us not trifle away this gift from God by allowing the deceiver to suggest to us that our cross to bear is a sickness or a sorrow or one of the myriad other of life's risks or problems. To do so is but to mask the necessary choices that each of us must continually make for finding life. No! Sicknesses, problems, and the like are only the circumstances that come to all lives that set the stage for the images that we choose to project. The only real drama is the one that finds us resolving these "opportune time" experiences through examining our emotions and feelings boldly and in the light of Love's image, nailing what is destructive and false of the choices before us to a cross to die, thereby denying one more time that one who always waits for us in life's shadows.

One other image proclaims the Give-away in a clear and demonstrative way that is helpful to us. It is the sacrament called the Eucharist. At the heart of the community life of Jesus' disciples was the command to remember him. Experienced by the original twelve on the occasion of the last Passover meal shared with the teacher before his crucifixion, his words, and their association with specific actions involving bread and wine became the basic, foundational act of devotion that has kept his life continuous and present in Christian communities down through the centuries. St. Paul provides the earliest written documentation of this rite. In his letter to the church in Corinth, he writes:

— *"The teaching I gave you was given me personally by the Lord himself, and it was this: the Lord Jesus, in the same night in which he was betrayed, took bread and when he had given thanks he broke it and said, 'Take, eat, this is my body which is being broken for you. Do this in remembrance of me.' Similarly, when supper was ended, he took the cup saying, 'This cup is the new agreement in my blood: do this, whenever you drink it, in remembrance of me.'"*[162]

Sadly, the Church has argued and flagellated itself over this sacrament for centuries. Like the loss of a lifestyle in favor of a next-life projection that began in the fourth century, here, also, I believe, has the early Church's experience of a daily embrace of the image of Love and its accompanying Way been misdirected into something that is far less than the witness of the give-away.

How do you hear? Step by step, let us look at what the sacrament proclaims.

— *"Take, eat. Drink it."*

Become one with the bread, with the wine. Let it be in you, let it be your very life. Like all food that we eat, let it be the nourishment that creates who you are and gives life to your body. This fits well in the vision of imaging the living God. It fits the Lord's statement about the Comforter, *"I am not going to leave you alone in the world—I am coming to you."*[163] Paul understood it perfectly and proclaimed it as the mystery now revealed: *"Christ in us, the hope of Glory."*[164] Eat. Drink. One, perfectly one.

— *"This is my body which is being broken for you... This is the new agreement in my blood."*

For generations beyond numbering, the mysterious temple rite had annually exhibited and portrayed this very thing. Two animals, perfect in life and similar in looks, were led to the temple courts. The once-a-year presentation of their lives as bearers of sin through the breaking of flesh and offering of blood resealed the ancient Covenant promises between Israel and God. Now, Jesus proclaimed a new agreement, a new Covenant relationship between humanity and the Almighty, that would come through his torn body, sealed with the covering of his shed blood. How wondrous! Surely, the disciples sensed the drama of it all. The Christ's blood: in it, with it, through it, humanity became acceptable finally, eternally, with its Creator. He offered there his body to us, for us. This, too, fits perfectly with the eternal revelation of God's image.

— *"Do this in remembrance of me, when you eat and drink."*

Something that we do regularly, that is the common, daily experience and need of us all—eating and drinking—as often as we do it, we are to remember him. The early community of believers did just that:

— *"... they continued steadily... in the breaking of the bread... day by day they met by common consent in the temple; they broke bread together in their homes, sharing meals with simple joy."*[165]

How necessary it was and is to act out repetitively those things that we want finally to do without thinking. "Day by day... breaking bread... remembering." However, somewhere during the years thereafter, a change came in. Could it be linked to the change occasioned by Constantine's conversion or could it have happened earlier when the first generation of disciples and believers, the eyewitnesses to the Christ, began to die and it was left to the recorders of the story to convey the Way that was to be the life of the Body?

Who knows? But listen again to what Jesus said: "Do this...." Do what? Break bread, drink wine? Is that it? Sit at the table, get up and go to work, and remember that Jesus died, died on a cross as the atoning sacrifice? Is that the work of, "Do this!", to proclaim that Jesus offered his life as the image of the Unseen Creator who is Love? Is it just to take the bread and drink the wine and leave the table saying, "Thank you, Lord Jesus, for doing this for me!"

Listen closely now to these next words of the apostle so that we can hear what he teaches about the Eucharist in the context of The Way that the early community of believers lived and witnessed Christ before the world.

— *"This can only mean that whenever you eat this bread or drink of this cup, you are proclaiming that the Lord has died for you, and you will do that until he comes again."*[166]

The disciples were taught specifically by Jesus to live and replicate his teaching and example everywhere they went. They were to speak the things he spoke, do the things he did, be the life he was and would forever be. He had left them an example, not of an act (the foot washing) but of a life (servant-hood).

— *"Believe me, the servant is not greater than his master and the messenger is not greater than the man who sent him. Once you have realized these things, you will find your happiness in doing them."*[167]

Picking up one's cross, following Jesus' daily examples, fulfilling the disciple-life, teaching what the master instructed, proclaiming the kingdom's presence, enjoining to ourselves the give-away life and the way of the cross: all were and are involved in "do this." It is in the breaking of the self-seeking nature of our own lives to give life to those around us, in the offering of our own life-substance as a covering for any and all whose inner holy-of-holies has become overwhelmed by the shadows of their world, that the image of the Christ, of Love, comes again and again in each new day. This drives away fear and despair and raises to new life those amongst our human family who have been living as those who are dead.

The Eucharist is not an act of doing the mass so as to receive a gift that has no personal cost. Rather, it is an expression of our own personal participation with Christ in a discipled community, portrayed in the give-away experience, the offering of self one hundred percent and asking zero percent in return. It is our own personal way of the cross. Said in the first person, it is my body and my blood, now offered in and with Christ in order to make the image of Love known in my day, in my world, so that others might see him come again and at last find their own lives. We in truth, re-member him in our own flesh. He who was broken, dis-membered, for us now returns again in our day, re-membered wherever two or three or more ."...*gather together in my name.*"[168]

— *"The fields. are ripe for harvest! Laborers are few! Who will go? Count the*

cost! You will drink the cup that I drink and share my baptism. Do you love me? Then feed my lambs, care for my sheep, you feed them."[169]
Here am I, Lord; send me.

C. Not by might, nor by power: a solitary journey.

One of the fundamental truths of scripture is that God's revelation of Self is a corporate affair. We are made for relationships and our true life is found in community where Love can be seen and shared. Genesis recorded that we were created in the image of God by the words, "*...in the image of God he created **him**, male and female he created **them**.*" Abram's call to covenant was in the promise of God that he would become, "*...a great nation... as the stars of heaven and the sand which is on the seashore.*" Israel, the seed of Abraham's flesh, did indeed become a great nation of twelve tribes. The covenant of God, first made with Abraham, continued with the nation, not with individuals. The new covenant with the Eternal One, made in the shed blood of Jesus, was "*...for you (the twelve disciples) and for many.*" Scripture teaches us that when Jesus was lifted upon the cross, "*...all men were drawn to himself,*" and that he prayed "*...for all those who will believe in me through their (the disciples') message, that they may all be one.*"

Paul's teaching on the mystery of being "*...all baptized by the Spirit into one body, whether we were Jews or Greeks, slaves or free men... for we are all members one of another...*" and his teaching on how the "*...dividing walls of hostility*" are broken down making "*...one body in place of the two,*" gives further witness to the truth that the image of God is seen in relationships and not in any individual experience of life apart from the community. And yet, even in this truth, the father of lies has come to create an image in the Church that has caused a history of pain and sorrow rather than the reconciling peace of God that passes all understanding.[170]

Evangelism of the world for Christ has been a part of the faith community from the very beginning of the New Testament experience. In our contemporary world, the evangelical banner is waved emblazoned with the words, "Go ye out into all the world and baptize," and Christians go out from the street corner to the jungles to win souls for heaven in the conviction that it is our Great Commission to do so. But a long history of evangelical witness precedes us, so it may be best that we try to find a base from which to weigh our judgments and decisions and work from there.

Somewhere along the way (again, might it be linked to the early fourth century's transformation of religious experience in the Roman world?), the witness of a community's way of life which was so attractive and so inviting that others who lived near by could see and touch the life of that community and want naturally to be a part of it, that witness came to an end. As that happened, the witness was replaced by a Church that heard the words of the risen Jesus from the perspective of positions of privilege and power. Their words now reflected an interpretation mirroring the theology of dualism that portrayed eternal life beyond the grave in terms of heaven or hell.

A different motive for building the community of faith seems to have sprung up. No longer was the Church willing to lose all for the hope of changing this world through the image of the risen Christ and his Love. Now, it began to struggle to maintain and increase the control and strength of those communities and/or persons that had risen to positions of authority and worldly power. Control all too often became the key rather than Love. Judgment became the message rather than acceptance. Fear became the method rather than peace and freedom.

The ensuing centuries of theological development spawned a sad pottage that is far removed from the wondrous image of,

— *"one loaf, one cup, one body, one Spirit, one hope, one Lord, one faith, one baptism, one God and Father of us all."*[171]

Out of the loss of a living community committed to Love's give-away and dedicated to witness to the resurrection of the Christ in one's flesh and the Kingdom's resultant presence, came a faith which interpreted heaven as being a place beyond the grave, the attainment of which was linked to merely being baptized into Christ (and that according to a host of interpretations, rules, and loyalties). The result: the development of all manner of divisive theologies, communities, and experiences. Examples (short list):

— An enduring legacy of anti-Semitism;
— The infamous experience of the Inquisitions;
— The Crusades;
— The medieval Religious Wars and contemporary religious civil strife;
— The abuses and disobedience of an imperial Catholic Church;
— The division of Christendom into political, geographical, competing denominations;
— The legacy of support for and empowering of a history of colonialism and its resulting eradication of cultures and peoples world-wide;
— The history of racial and sexual bondage that only now is being addressed;
— And more.

But it is enough to stop with such listing. To go on would leave one thinking that the heritage of Christ's life and passion has done little good for the world we have become and that is far from the truth. The community of believers has offered (and continues to be) a fountain of compassion and mercy, always maintaining even in the worst moments of its own witness, a hopeful image of the Creator. Because of the Church, we are here to tell this story and offer its redeeming message.

What we who claim the Name of Christ for ourselves need to learn about the presence and attainment of the promised land is that it is not by power, nor by might, that this kingdom of our God is attained. Let me say that again. It is not by power, or manipulation, or methods of control, or judgment, or fear, or threats, that the kingdom of heaven is attained. Moreover, it is not the calling of the disciples of the Christ to go out and coerce, win, or make anyone into anything for God. Nowhere in the plan of creation is there anything assigned by the Creator to the created except to image the Almighty, the One who is Eternal Love. In that image, serve. That's all. And that is enough!

We have never been given a commission nor do we have the right in Christ to change (or try to change) anyone either by force, or by politic or by judgment. The Christ is quite clear about it. *"What must we do to carry out the work of God?"*

— *"...believe in the one whom he has sent to you."*[172]

And again:

— *"Don't criticize people, and you will not be criticized. For you will be judged by the way you criticize others, and the measure you give will be the measure you receive. Why do you look at the speck of sawdust in your brother's eye and fail to notice the plank in your own? How can you say to your brother, 'Let me get the speck out of your eye,' when there is a plank in your own? You fraud! Take the plank out of your own eye first, and then you can see clearly enough to remove your brother's speck of dust."*[173]

Each of us, individually, has one responsibility and one alone, and that is to be the image of God in our own journey and in our own environment and community and in our own personality. Everyone else's work and responsibility is theirs alone. We are not to judge them for their journey nor figure out some way to make them accept and join ours. It is a singular, individual experience with the One who loves and redeems us in the atonement of the Christ, found and manifested in the midst of the community of all creation: individual life in the embrace of communal experience. This is a mystery, maybe a manifestation of being created *". . . in the image of God he created him; male and female he created them."* I, the individual, am called to live with you, the community, in the image of our mutual Creator who, by my knowledge and acceptance of Christ's fellowship in me, bids me only to love and serve you in a Way called The Giveaway. Whether you do it or not. Whether you accept me or reject me. Whether anyone else in all creation does it or not. Each of us was created individually and redeemed personally only to be the image of God in this world in the presence of our brothers and sisters. Nothing more. And, nothing less.

— *"So he said, 'Yes, Lord, but what about him?'*
If it is my wish,' returned Jesus, 'for him to stay until I come, is that your business, Peter? You must follow me.'"[174]

— *"...So you also, when you have done all that is commanded you, say, 'We are unworthy servants; we have only done what was our duty.'"*[175]

CHAPTER RECAP:

The kingdom of God is now, here, on this side of the grave and in our very midst. It is within us! Each of us. It is so because it is where the King of Creation has come to dwell, able to do so through the merits of the atoning sacrifice of the Lamb of God, the Christ.

How do we live in the kingdom? We live by Love in the present moment. Living this way is the full image of God; God is Love. But there is more to it than simply saying the words. Love is the servant-life of sacrifice for the sake of the world in which we dwell. Called *The Way of the Cross* or the *Give-away*, it is the expression of our personal choice to enter freely into every relationship of our journey, from the closest and most intimate to the brief encounter with the stranger or sojourner, with full and equal compassion and righteousness.

Our love is never coercive or controlling nor does it act from a position of judgment and/or condemnation. The kingdom life of Love is a solitary journey that demands only our own best efforts to make the Eternal One known in the midst of the communities of our world. Like leaven added to the bread of life, like salt spread upon the meal, we individually are called just to be who we are in Christ and let the witness, the image, be God's work and will for others. It is the Creator who shall call His creation through us and give life through the image we might show. It is important for us to know, however, that unless that image is made known, there shall never be the restoration of the paradise for which we all long.

CHAPTER SEVEN
LIVING IN ETERNITY

Have you realized yet that you are the promised land, that you do not have to wait to get to eternal life someday but that Eternal Life already exists in you waiting for you to enjoy and to fathom the depths of the richness of His Love for you there? Have you made it to your promised land? Has it sunk home? God, the Creator of your life who loved you in the beginning with a Love that is eternal, dwells in you! The Eternal King of glory dwells within you and has therein established the kingdom of heaven in you. Do you understand it?

In truth, the Christ has revealed it for us all and established it sure and strong. Jesus and his willing sacrifice of his own life nearly two thousand years ago accomplished and made known what most all the religions of the world over most all of time have endeavored to see: he reconciled the whole creation back to its Creator and restored the presence of paradise back to the earth. He is for all of us the way home to God. His image reveals all that is true about our nature, and the life he shared in every relationship fully portrays the life for which humanity was created.

— *"Go your way; your sins are forgiven... If the Son, then, sets you free, you are really free... Believe me when I tell you that if anybody accepts my words, he will never see death (separation) at all... you will realize that I am in my Father, that you are in me, and I am in you."*[176]

Is there anything else, then, for us in this journey of *Getting to the Promised Land*? Yes. There is the need to talk of living in Eternity. Those of us who know the presence of God and know the freedom of living in the image of Love have come to accept the reality that such knowledge and such freedom go hand in hand with the call to discipleship. There is not one without the other, and if you have accepted your inheritance then you have also accepted the truth that there is a personal cost to it and that cost is the Giveaway, the Way of the Cross. It is the disciple's life. Freedom to be truly alive is wed to discipleship.

In this chapter, we will look together at the disciple's life, some new ways of thinking about the kingdom of heaven, and a more faithful definition of the Church that might restore to it the wonder and the Spirit of the first faith community. We will come to know what it means to live in such a way as to elude death forever and see paradise restored. How to start? Let us use Jesus' words to the new covenant community which witnesses to the truth of his atoning passion, the words that start them on their way in the kingdom:

— *"All power in Heaven and on earth has been given to me. You, then, are to go and make disciples of all the nations and baptize them in the name of the Father and of the Son and of the Holy Spirit. Teach them to observe all that I have commanded you and, remember, I am with you always, even to the end of the world."*[177]

A. *All Power—in heaven, on earth—belongs to Love.*

Jesus grew and matured in the knowledge that he had power. The first glimpse shared with us in the Gospels is the story of his temptation in the wilderness. On one level of looking at this story, we would have to acknowledge that Jesus did nothing. No miracles, no changing something into something else; just wandering, sitting alone in the wilderness with the companionship of his own inner thoughts. Yet it is precisely there, visited within by the spirits that come to us all, that Jesus came to know the true measure of Love's power and how to exercise it in a pure and holy image. There, he saw, he heard, his Father's presence even as the shadow-spirit's lure welled up alongside; and he chose to act out Love's life. It became in him the realization of power to live in the shadow of death and have no fear; there, with the knowledge of God's presence within him, angelic "staffs" anointed him and set before him an overflowing cup of peace. In that place where heaven and earth were joined, there in the firstborn of all creation, Love's power was made manifest and all that was fallen and distorted in the revealing of God's image was rejected by the inheritance given to the Son of man in his birth.

From that beginning, the Gospels, all four of them, speak of Jesus' use of this power to affect in some fashion, the lives of those around him. Referred to most frequently as miracle stories, the portrayal of Jesus' daily living reveals relationships with all sorts and conditions of men and women who bear the contents found in the relationships of us all and who bring to every moment their experiences of brokenness, dis-ease of mind and body, and social disarray. It is unfortunate that most often we read the Gospels as if Jesus had a daily game-plan to deal with these things:

— "Today I'll feed a bunch of people, raise a dead man, and work on the relationships of James and John with the rest of the disciples. Then lunch and a short nap. At mid-day, we'll go to the lake and I'll put a boat out a bit from shore and share a few parables. Dinner is at seven with Zacchaeus, then it's off to Mary and Martha's for a good night's sleep."

It wasn't that way. Like us all, Jesus began each day in the awareness that it would present a mix of success and failure, fulfilled dreams and dashed hopes, peace and turmoil, all wrapped up together in a package of risk and uncertainty. Life in the flesh in a fallen creation was, and is, one of chance and unfair, random experiences; rain falls on the just and the unjust equally. None of us, not even Jesus, has final, full control of the events that make up our days. Each future moment is unknown, waiting to happen in the midst of our journey, and only our response to what occurs gives us opportunity to reveal the presence of the indwelling Redeemer whose image has power to heal and renew these moments. What makes the story of Jesus such Good News for us is that he, though like us in not having a foreknowledge of what was to occur, nonetheless responded to each day's events in such a way as to reveal Love's power in the circumstances of those with whom he related, causing them to marvel,

— *"Could this be the One for whom we have waited? He speaks and acts with authority, not like the scribes."*[178]

How attractive and riveting is Love's image when it is seen and felt consistently for the first time!

But, there is a strange attribute about our humanity in its fallenness that seems to lead us always to focus on the gift rather than the Giver. We want the effects without Love's motivation. There is a story from the life of the early church about a magician named Simon.

— *"When he saw how the Spirit was given through the apostles' laying their hands upon people, he offered them money with the words, 'Give me this power too, so that if I were to put my hands on anyone he could receive the Holy Spirit.' But Peter said to him, 'To hell with you and your money! How dare you think you can buy the gift of God!... your heart is not honest with God... for I see inside you, and I see a man bitter with jealousy and bound with his own sin.'"*[179]

Jesus had taught his disciples it is not the things on the outside that make one unclean or defiled. No, our problem of image comes from elsewhere: from within. He taught,

— *"...whatever comes out of a man, that is what makes a man... unclean. For it is from inside, from men's hearts and minds, that evil thoughts arise... All these evil things come from inside a man and make him unclean."*[180]

It is so much easier to settle for cheap grace rather than the gift that comes with and from the Cross!

Paul also dealt clearly with this idea of seeking a lesser image than that of the Holy One. Speaking to the Gentiles who were not taught for generations in the Covenants of Israel and who were not recipients of the insights of the Hebrew prophets, he said that nonetheless even they ought to have acknowledged the Almighty, that they were without excuse for their wickedness:

— *"For since the beginning of the world the invisible attributes of God, e.g. his eternal power and divinity, have been plainly discernible through things which he has made and which are commonly seen and known... yet... these men became just fools, fools who would exchange the glory of the immortal God for an imitation image... they gave up God...*"[181]

From cheap grace comes cheap worship that results in a cheap portrayal of the image of Love in our common life.

All too often we, too, would rather focus on the **results** of the loving relationships Jesus entered into, as if the **results** were the issue and the full truth of God's power in him. We are amazed that he walked on water, healed lepers, made a few loaves of bread feed thousands. Wanting the **results**, we try the faith life for a while in the hopes that it will bring forth in us the same manifestations of power. Living in the thought that because we are believers, no problems shall come to us, and more so that we shall prosper in this world even as sinners fall, we are devastated when sickness pays its inevitable visit or the arbitrary randomness of pain and suffering are inflicted upon us or the ones for whom we pray. "How can it be? I am a Christian!" We pray for healing and sickness grows worse. We pray for peace and wars intensify. We pray for poverty and prejudice and evil to flee before our prayers and soon the very things we prayed would end come to dwell even within our walls. *"Give us bread! We want more of the bread!"*

Have we not heard yet that the gift, the only power, **is the Giver**, the *"true bread that comes down from heaven and gives life to the world?"*[182] Love is the inheritance that comes to the temple of our own bodies and becomes the bridegroom in the marriage with our souls. The Eternal One, ruling in the kingdom of our lives, exhibits not magic in a real world but rather the image of all that creates and re-creates: Love. The power of the invisible God at work in the Incarnate Christ, Jesus, went about embracing all as brother and sister, taking time to be family with those who were cast out of the family of man, bringing hope and comfort to those who were diseased by the pain and sin of the world, releasing legions of the beloveds from the bondage and shackles of their fears and sorrows. Love does that. The miracle is not in the result but rather in the expression of the image of God that brings the result! The inheritance—the gift, the promise—is the Eternal Life (which is Love) in us, *the hope of our glory!*

All power in heaven, in the flesh of Jesus, was also the power imaged through Jesus, on earth. It was, all of it, given to him!

B. *Go and make disciples of all the nations and baptize them.*

In order to truly come to grips with living in the kingdom and exercising the power of the inheritance in which we are born, portraying the image of the Lord with compassion and mercy, we have to understand the idea of discipleship. Notice here that the risen Christ did not say, "Go out and win souls for heaven, baptizing them in the name..." Rather, he said, "Go and make disciples..." There is a tremendous difference in the instruction he gave and how we have interpreted it, and in the effect and the result of our responses.

Disciple: one who is just like his/her teacher or master. Just like![183] Not sort-of-like nor a-believer-in. *One who is just like*! To see the disciple is to see the master who has called forth and taught the disciple. To see one is to see the other; to know one is to know the other. The disciple images the master. They are one. When Jesus called forth the twelve to be his disciples, he began the process of revealing himself, his very life, to them, so that by what he taught them and what he showed them, they could be just like him when he sent them out. The process of imaging is all wrapped up in the work of discipling; the process and the result are the same. Some Old Covenant examples help here:

— Joseph made the will of pharaoh known, speaking pharaoh's wishes and proclaiming his commands. To see one was to know the other.

— Moses pleaded with God to spread the load of leadership (it was too much for him to do alone). God took some of the Spirit that was on Moses and gave it to seventy elders of the people, even to two who were in the camp at the time of the Spirit's visitation. To see them was to be under the leadership of Moses.

— Elisha received a double portion of the spirit of Elijah and when he came to the band of disciples they proclaimed, "The spirit of Elijah has fallen on Elisha!" To see one was to see the other.

When Jesus told his followers that, ." . . to see me is to see the Father," he was leading them forthrightly into the same understanding of discipleship that he proclaimed in the resurrection exhortation to them. In this final statement before he leaves them, he is saying,

— "Go to all the nations and reveal my image there. Be my disciples wherever you go that others might know me, and through me, know and image the Eternal One. Make them into disciples of yourself just as I made you disciples of myself and just as I have been the presence of the Living Eternal One. Let us all be one, perfectly the same."[184]

How different the disciple is from a believer! Many believed that Jesus was the Christ. Even the demons that dwelt in Legion the madman believed it! But believing and becoming are two different things.

For the past seventeen centuries (maybe even longer) and certainly today, most all of the baptized community have believed in God, believed that Jesus is the Son of God, and confessed Jesus as their Lord and Savior. Yet, many have neither accepted the call to be his disciples nor accepted the truth that they are to be just like him in image and in lifestyle. Moreover, we are taught quite plainly that only Jesus is God in human flesh, and that he alone lives the image of God Incarnate while the rest of humanity are sinners in human flesh and can neither deny our sins nor live free of them in this life. "It is not possible for us to be just like Jesus!" say far too many of the Church.

What we are then teaching is that Jesus' command and Great Commission to his disciples was impossible and that we could not present in and through our lives the image of our teacher. Hence, we have accepted something far less in the command, something greatly distorted in the image, and made it to be a means of dividing and identifying the family of man under categories of saved and unsaved, spirit-filled and damned, won and lost.

Hear it plainly: "*You, then, are to go and make disciples of all the nations...*" Nothing more is asked and certainly nothing less!

— "*A disciple is not above his teacher, but when he is fully trained, he will be like his teacher... what is good enough for the teacher is good enough for the disciple as well... I tell you truly that anyone who accepts my messenger will be accepting me, and anyone who accepts me will be accepting the one who sent me... He and I are one... Father, make them one even as we are one....*"[185]

Disciples. Baptize *them*.

Baptism is not the believer's entrance-ticket into heaven or the mark of a reconciled walk with God. Baptism is the expression of one's conscious choice of putting the old way-of-life to an end (separating it from our personal experiences and living-choices, putting it to death) and accepting the image of the Christ as one's own and the Way of the Cross as the expression of Love as the life one will now endeavor to live. One does not need baptism either as a proof-text or a work for salvation. Apart from a commitment to a new way of living, baptism means nothing and affects nothing. It certainly does not impress the Almighty or get the attention of the Firstborn. In these early days of the twenty-first century, baptism no longer even affects the energy of the local Body of Christ as more and more people see Christian faith only as a societal location for the rituals of hatching, matching, and dispatching. I once sat in the presence of a wise and loving Benedictine abbot who characterized the sad trends in the modern Church as leading it to be but a "marrying and burying society."

It needn't be this way! If we unlock some of the restrictions of our teaching and the definitions we apply to the doctrines and creeds that shape our heritage, maybe we can restore meaning to our own baptisms and our living in eternity. For instance, we have inherited a definition of salvation that focuses its meaning exclusively on one's entrance into a right relationship with God through the saving merits of Jesus' death on the cross. The way to salvation in the presence of God is through repentance of sin, acceptance of Jesus' death for me, and being baptized in water in a Trinitarian formula with a personal, verbal confession of Jesus as Lord and Savior. To do so means that one is *saved* and will spend eternity with Jesus in heaven before the throne of God. To deny the process is to be labeled as *lost* and to be seen as one who will spend eternity in hell with all the sinners of the universe, there to be in torment at the hands of the devil. "Brother, sister: are you saved?"

It somehow seems offensive to me to find the evangelical pamphlet, *Five Easy Steps to Salvation*, placed on the top of the rest-room urinal. I think Jesus would be saddened that his witness is reduced to such a charade. Salvation, in truth, is the result of one's movement from places of bondage in one's life to places of freedom and release. Such movements happen over and over again in our journey through life and we win and lose our salvation continually, depending on our response to the chances, risks, and experiences that are presented to us. We are saved and/or lost over and over again as we live and mature, succeed and fail. Moreover, our life in the kingdom within each of us is like, for example, an onion. We come to grips with the top layer of our journeys, finally freeing ourselves from disobedience and at last reflecting the image of Love. Then, circumstances change and reveal in us another layer, something different in our character that is a dimmed reflection of Grace, and we start afresh on the journey to be saved from this taint on our soul. Finally, salvation comes, freedom again is ours. Then, in life, another layer revealed; and later, another; and another. And so through the whole journey of life. Ever going deeper and deeper into the fullness of life in the kingdom. The image—saved and lost, again and again. Sanctification is the experiential process of working out the life of Christ, our salvation, in us day by day. Peter exhorted the first community of converts with these words:

— *"Save yourselves from this perverted generation!"*[186]

Paul encouraged the Church in this way:

— *"So then, my dearest friends, as you have always followed my advice... so now... work out the salvation that God has given you with a proper sense of awe and responsibility. For it is God who is at work within you, giving you the will and power to achieve his purpose."*[187]

We are all, each of us, participants in the work and process of our own salvation on a daily basis. It is not a work of fear or done in the threat of losing the fellowship of Love. The Eternal One is with us, the Christ is in us, the inheritance of the Spirit is ours forever, working with us and longing to achieve our complete freedom through the purpose and power of God. It is Love's will.

Let us use a better word from the early community of believers to describe the effect of Christ's passion and its relationship to our fellowship with the Almighty in the kingdom. It is a word far more faithful to describing the work that gets us to the promised land and truer to the description of Love's eternal purpose and will. The word is reconciliation. If death describes our separation from God due to the deceiver's first image of disobedience and sin, then the life of Love imaged for us and in us in the Christ must describe our reconciliation. The opposite of separation is reconciliation, not salvation! What was once lost is found, what was once divided by an impassable gulf has been reunited by a straight highway through the desert. The blood of the

89

lamb of God has covered the world and reconciled the new Covenant people to their Creator. Listen to the teaching of the early Church:

— *"The very spring of our actions is the love of Christ. We look at it like this: if one died for all men then, in a sense, they all died, and his purpose in dying for them is that their lives should now be no longer lived for themselves but for him who died and rose again for them... All this is God's doing, for he has reconciled us to himself through Jesus Christ; and he has made us agents of the reconciliation. God was in Christ personally reconciling the world to himself—not counting their sins against them—and has commissioned us with the message of reconciliation... For God caused Christ, who himself knew nothing of sin, actually to be sin for our sakes, so that in Christ we might be made good with the goodness of God."*[188]

Is it clear enough? What was separated from God (by God) and cast forth from paradise so the image of disobedience would never inherit what was Eternal, has now been reconciled to God (by God) for the very purpose of Love being inherited by the creation and Christ imaged, that He might be "all in all."[189] If I might say it one more time from the scriptures so that the distinction is clear and bright, it would be this from the teaching of Paul:

— *"Yet the proof of God's amazing love is this: that it was while we were yet sinners that Christ died for us. Moreover, if he did that for us while we were sinners, now that we are men justified by the shedding of his blood, what reason have we to fear the wrath of God? If, while we were his enemies, Christ reconciled us to God by dying for us, surely now that we are reconciled we may be perfectly certain of our salvation through his living in us!"*[190]

Reconciliation first, then comes the hope of salvation. God affects the work of reconciliation in the Christ for us; with the Spirit of Christ, we work out the Savior's life (we image it) in us. Here, then, is the Good News, the Gospel: the whole cosmos and everything in it is reconciled to the Creator and the Eternal One indwells it all forever; nothing is lost or separated from God! Reconciliation and redemption is complete, once and for all. The work of living in eternity is that of saving ourselves from "this perverted generation," which is also the decision to enter into the community of disciples, which makes all who seek to image the inheritance of Love the agents of Christ's reconciliation in every moment of living.

These, then, the ones who seek to image the Lord and who are willing to answer the call of discipleship for the sake of the work in the world of making Love's image known, these are the ones who shall signal that call through the rite of baptism and their participation in the life of Christ's body, the Church. I suspect that when we get boldly honest about this, the Church in all its present diversity may begin to reconcile first itself, and then, though much smaller, become the teaching community that it was always meant to be. To that, we now turn.

C. *Teach them to observe all that I have commanded you.*

The Church, the Body of the Christ in the world, is the training arena, the practice ground, where the discipled community makes perfect in their own lives the teachings of the Christ. It is a replicated process that finds its origins in the ministry of Jesus himself. From the beginning when John the Baptist's disciples left him and went to see what he meant when he said,

— *"There is the lamb of God... I declare publicly before you all that he is the Son of God,"*[191]

Jesus' answer to all who inquired of his identity and his mission was essentially the same:

— *"Come and see."*[192]

And come, they did. Leaving the known for the unknown, his following grew. The core community around Jesus left everything and devoted themselves to being disciples. They traveled wherever Jesus went, listened to his public teachings and probed privately his parable's hidden meanings, learned the life of Love and its healing grace, and even went out on selected missions in Jesus' name to practice what they had so far learned. Over and over they were taught a new way of living, in keeping with the life of their fathers and their father's fathers yet different in that what they learned was to become not a thing of the head but a life of the heart: a one hundred percent life of imaging everything about this man, their Christ. Failures were many and their old habits were constantly revealed as relationships became strained. Forgiveness became a matter of central importance, indeed the heart of the Love they were witnessing and learning to image.

— *"Master, how many times can my brother wrong me and I must forgive him? Would seven times be enough?"*

"No," replied *Jesus, "not seven times, but seventy times seven!"*[193]

Lessons on forgiveness abounded in the fellowship for in all human relationships there are slights and times of stress. The world teaches us to run or fight in such moments, but Jesus was teaching the disciples to forgive, and in forgiveness to maintain the unity of the relationships in the bonds of reconciliation and the Spirit of Love. Forgiveness and reconciliation embodies the image and it must be portrayed if anyone else is to learn how to live it. Nothing is unforgivable in the fellowship except maybe unforgiveness, for it alone is opposite to, the absolute negative reflection of, the Spirit which is the inheritance for the flesh, the life of Love.[194] We must forgive every slight and debt and sin, acknowledging in the act of forgiveness that we do not count the action or the moment or the experience against this one in whom we know the presence of the Creator to dwell, no matter how poorly Love might be revealed there.

None of this life of forgiveness (of Love) comes to us easy. We are all well taught in the ways of separation, all poorly taught in the ways of the Spirit. Perfection takes practice, in loving as in anything else done in the flesh. Think about it. To play the piano, to make the works of the masters come alive through our own hands, takes practice, hours and hours of disciplined practice. To be a skilled surgeon and restore to wholeness the lives of those whose bodies have been broken by disease or violence takes years and years of practice. To be a skilled athlete, a competent farmer, a valued mechanic: all take maturing through devoted, consistent, repetitive practice of the skill one wants to make not only one's own but one's very life. So with Love! The Body of The Christ, called the Church, is the place of practice for beginners in the presence of those who already are seasoned disciples of the Teacher. When we are

— *"...grow(n) up in every way into him who is the head, into Christ,... to mature manhood, to the measure of the stature of the fullness of Christ,"*[19]

then we shall naturally pass on to the next generation, the next neighbor, the image of life, and humbly with love extend the invitation, "Come and see." It is a process that is like leavening the loaf, or like seed growing in the ground, or like servants tending to another's household. We do it not for gain or reward but rather because it is the life that we were created to live. No matter if any one else ultimately sees or if any one else follows or not. It is not a life that is better than another's or one that is called to change anyone else's journey. It is simply learning and practicing and living the life we know to be ours, consistently and for its own calling.

"I must be about my Father's business. I am who I am."

CHAPTER RECAP:

The Church exists to teach disciples to be Christ in their world. It is a fellowship of commitment one to another that creates community wherever it exists. The common cup of the table; the remembering that is in truth the recreating of Love in the relationships of our fellowship; the Way of the Cross that practices and practices the Give-away to bring life to others; the life of serving from positions of humility that always counts others better than ourselves; the forgiveness that knows no bounds and is offered only in the knowledge that to withhold it destroys the inheritance that alone gives us life; and the self-control that hides nothing from others nor from the self in its utter confidence in God's Promise: all this is the inheritance from the Risen Jesus that was the fullness of life in the early community called the Church. It is still the life you and I can share in the inheritance of our own promised lands and the gift that God bids us to image to our Covenant family, the world. Wherever you and I find it made manifest, there is the Church as it was created to be. My prayer as we come to the end of this journey is that we find it, you and I, in the arenas of our own lives. Or lacking it, we create it in the midst of the fellowships we share. Ultimately, you and I have but one choice in it all, and that is to be ourselves in the fullness of the kingdom of God wherever we are, trusting that the image of the Eternal One in us will grow and will attract others to Love's image, embracing it in their own new birth.

REPRISE

Thank you. I am humbled that you chose to pursue the journey that I have put to print. When I started writing *Getting to the Promised Land*, it was as a discipline-project for the quiet summer months, something to frame each day and make me continue pondering the faith experiences I was trying to share with others.

"What is real for me in the Christian faith?" was (and still is) a constant question as I exercise my vocation as a priest. If what I did and said was not real, not alive, and part of the everyday stuff of my journey, then I did not want to go through the rituals or the routines, either for my sake or for the sake of the flock committed to my care. The faith confessed and experienced in the sanctuary had to be, must be, the same expression of living that happens in the home, the workplace, the social scene, etc. If not, something is a charade and I want no part of it, whether it be the daily experience or the activity of the Church.

So, in that summer now many years past, I started trying to put in print what I believed and what motivated my ministry and my life. I did it for my own sake. It is still the impulse behind my intentions no matter where this work ultimately lands or how many or few ever read it. In this last chapter, the Reprise, I share with you somewhat personally the things important to me about living one's short reflection of the human journey in the implications of the Kingdom.

Love is the key and relationships are everything. In the bonds of human companionship, indeed in the companionship of every living thing on the face of the earth, plant and animal, how we live out these relationships is all that matters. From beginning to end, from start to finish, from birth to the grave—the expression of our being together in the journey is the underlying impulse of existence. In and through the whole of it, Love is the key. If Love is present and is the bond that energizes the experience, life blossoms and nourishes everyone and everything. Beauty is seen and created, brightening the path we all share and expanding all the senses. Fear has no root and finds no field in which to grow; sorrow and loneliness fade from memories because they have nothing upon which to feed or multiply. Love is the beginning and the ending, the all in all of the heart (indeed, of everything).

I know, now, that I have always been loved. It has not always been a conscious part of my journey though, for I remember a time in my youth probably similar to most of us, a time of immaturity and selfish choices that I know brought injury and sorrow to others. I remember choices made because I needed, I wanted, I thought I did not have something; what, I did not know. Like everyone else, I looked outside my own journey to others and to things to satisfy this need. In the process, I used things and institutions and experiences as all consumers do, and I used people. I am so sorry and have asked the Creator for forgiveness. I have asked forgiveness from others where possible, and I have looked within with forgiveness to face the wilderness that required my absolute attention in order to finally get on with living. To all though, then and now, I say for the first time or finally, for my own health (and maybe for yours), "I am sorry for not loving *you* and I ask you to forgive me." I believe it necessary for me to do this in order to fulfill all righteousness (and I leave that for you to ponder along your own journey). But now in these later years, as I look back, I do so with the knowledge that I have always been loved. When my name was first "spoken," when my soul came into its being, when the Creator created me and the genetic stuff of my mother and father in the flesh came together, from before even then, I was loved. It leaves me in awe, almost breathless. Me! Loved! Not because of, not for this or that reason, not out of demand or manipulation or pleading—just loved. I was, am, will always be loved. Michael—loved of God. "Way down in my middle," as my family has learned to express it, Love is; and it lives and labors to bring forth its good fruit in all seasons. Somehow along the passing of the years, I found the kingdom of God and knew I was home.

I came to know something else. It was, for me, the first real and true expression of the faith into which I was born, the Christian faith, and its discovery brought clearer meaning to my vocation as a priest in the Church. I cannot remember a time when I have not participated in the Christian community. From a young boy-soprano to college crucifer to Episcopal priest, I have been in the house of the Lord reciting the creeds and prayers that express the Gospel story. In this chaotic world, the Church has held me like a safe and sure anchor and, I am sure, focused my soul's search for identity. But the Church, for me, also acted to impede my life journey, for it, like everything else that exists, encouraged by word and experience and definition my looking outside myself for the satisfaction of the needs of my flesh and my soul. It participated, through its very structure, politic, and theology, in the nourishment of the selfishness that bound me in my own inner wilderness. As I read the stories, heard the teachings, struggled with the commands and commandments, prayed the prayers, and tried to be what *it* asked me to be, somehow all of that experience came to express a basic motivation of, "If

you do this, then you will find... If you do not do this, then you will get..."
"If... then! You will find... get...!"

Other than the fact that I may have struggled harder than my friends with guilt over activity shared in a worldly witness that was shaping us all, being Christian did not make me look any different than anyone else. The passing of years added to this observation as college, first job, and being on my own witnessed this fact in a more universal way. Very few people were truly being shaped by the Church in such a way as to distinguish Christians in the midst of the world in which we were to live as leaven and shepherds. By activity, *by image*, we all pretty much looked alike!

Please know that I am very conscious that generalizations like this are always dangerous and I acknowledge the reality that without the Church's witness, poor as it might have been down through the centuries and into the present, what kind of world would we have? What would humanity's witness be without two thousand years of Christian presence? I am just confessing here, in wrestling with my own experience, that I believe that selfishness and self-fulfillment was and continues to be the message that I see most proclaimed by the institutional Christian Church. Just like it is the message of the world in which we as the Church exist!

After many, many years in this wilderness, in the first years of my ordained ministry, the Eternal Spirit maneuvered my family and me into living in the shared lifestyle of Christian Community. As rector of a large, urban, wealthy, conservative, traditional parish, Love led us and a substantial number of other Christian brothers and sisters into a shared-life experience. For over eight years, we and as many as eight other families in our fellowship took people from the streets, the jails, and from experiences of pain and brokenness to live with us in our homes and share our life and journey. We began to learn the message of the Give-away in real life experiences and the Way-of-the-Cross in our own emotions and feelings. The learning process was the way of salvation taught from and mirrored in those stories "... observing all that I have commanded you." We tried to redeem the brokenness in all our lives out of the parables, the miracles, and the teachings portrayed in the Gospels and soon found out that the biblical stories were indeed our own stories and that the life of the Bible itself became our own history. Word and deed made one in biblical story could still be word and deed together today! We saw the image of the Almighty in the relationships of our fellowship and the life of the Church. Mind you, I am not saying that our life was without problems or that either the local church or the homes we lived in were perfected or models of eternal peace—far from it. I am saying, rather, that in this experience of community, the life of the Give-away and the Way-of-the-Cross became real; that Love—the Spirit, God—became real, and such reality was found in looking *within* at how each of us dealt with the relationships which we shared so personally and intimately. We were learning to love from Love's Spirit, and in that Love healing and peace and renewed hope and life were found. I began to understand how my faith and Christian upbringing could express itself in every experience and every relationship of my life's journey. The image is meant to be lived and it became the hope of my soul! I came home; my wilderness wandering was over.

My wife and I no longer live a shared-communal experience, and we have moved three times since those years as we have served the Church. We have never been led to that kind of sharing again. But, I have continued to understand the truth of the Cross in ever new experiences and have found new opportunities to have Love tried and tested to see how far within I can remain safe in the Kingdom. I have found that the deceiver, that author of shadows, always exists for me and evil's opportune times always come. Life, for me, is like a great personal game to see how full Love can be and how infinite is my personal experience of Eternity. Sometimes I feel victorious in the contest, the lesson (that layer of my life, like the example of the onion) is done with, and I see life in a new and exciting way. Then comes another of life's random moments and the process of confronting something within begins anew. Once, I feared these moments. But when I began to understand, to know, truly know, that I was and am and always will be loved, and that nothing will ever separate me from the Lover and Creator of my soul, fear stopped and the contest became only that, a contest. It is a contest that I cannot lose since the victory was won long ago and I was brought home safely in the arms of my Lord and Savior, Jesus, the Christ. The life I now lead is his life, for I am his disciple. Christ in me is the hope of my every day, and my prayer is that he might be seen in me by everyone. I know, however, that Love's image in me will not be the case in every circumstance for my frailties are many. More so, not everyone saw God clearly in Jesus either, who I, at least, acknowledge as perfect man. But if a few, my wife and my children, know Love in me; and if my children might see Love in and through the relationship of their parents; if through such a small window I might be used of Love to touch and leaven a singular, small part of eternity and share in the Creator's plan unfolding since "...in the beginning..." then I shall count everything worth the cost.

Welcome to the joy of the kingdom!
May it grow and grow within you in the
Love of the Christ.

NOTES

1. Exodus 34:7.
2. John 1:1-4
3. John 13:23
4. John 13:25
5. 1 John 4:8
6. Matthew 18:20
7. Exodus 3:11
8. Exodus 3:13-14
9. Luke 2:49
10. John 14:9
11. John 10:30
12. John 17:22
13. John 19:9
14. John 6:35; 8:12; 8:58; 10:7; 10:11; 11:25; 14:6; 15:1
15. Galatians 2:20
16. Luke 2:52
17. A combination from 1 Corinthians 2:12-17, 2 Corinthians 5:17-20, and Romans 8:14-17
18. A combination from Galatians 2:20 and Colossians 1:26-27
19. John 17:22
20. Acts 1:4
21. 2 Corinthians 5:21 (also refer to chapter 3 and the work of Atonement)
22. Genesis 2:15-17
23. See Revelation 12:7-17
24. Genesis 3:22
25. Romans 6:23
26. Romans 5:12
27. Psalm 5:15
28. See Exodus 19, Genesis 17, and Revelation 21
29. See Psalm 89:33-37
30. A combination of Ezekiel 34, Isaiah 53, Ezekiel 33 and Isaiah 7

31. Philippians 2:6-8
32. Matthew 27:46
33. Isaiah 25:7
34. John 11:49-52
35. John 19:30
36. Luke 23:46
37. Luke 23:46
38. 2 Corinthians 5:14
39. Romans 6:10
40. 2 Corinthians 5:19-21
41. Philippians 1:21-24
42. Isaiah 42:8
43. Taken from John 17
44. Philippians 2:5-8
45. Leviticus 16:34
46. Leviticus 16:21-22
47. See Genesis 15:6 and Romans 4:22-25
48. See also Hebrews 9:22
49. From Luke 14:7-14 and 21:1-4
50. A recurrent story, taken here from Deuteronomy 15:15 and 26:8
51. Exodus 12:11-23
52. Leviticus 17:11
53. Ezekiel 33
54. Ezeliel 34
55. Isaiah 49:3 and the "servant" passages ff.
56. Isaiah 49:6-8
57. Matthew 1:21
58. John 6:6-27
59. John 6:28-29
60. John 6:32-33
61. John 6:35,53-57
62. John 6:60
63. John 6:63
64. John 3:23
65. The understanding of John 6:51 and 1 Corinthians 11:24
66. John 11:50
67. John 11: 51-52
68. Matthew 26:28
69. Exodus 3:14
70. A combination of John 14:9 and John 10:30
71. From Exodus 19:5-6, 8
72. Exodus 19:8
73. Judges 3:7 and a repeated theme throughout the book of Judges

74. 2 Samuel 7:11-16
75. Jeremiah 7:4
76. Micah 6:6-8
77. Hosea 6:6
78. Genesis 18:22-33
79. A combination from Isaiah 6:13 and 11:1,10
80. Micah 5:2
81. Jeremiah 23:5-6
82. Ezekiel 34:23-24
83. Genesis 3:15
84. See Colossians 1:15 and Hebrews 1:3
85. Please look to Matthew 1:18-25, Luke 1:26-34, and John 1:1-18
86. St. Luke 2:40
87. Luke 2:29-32
88. Matthew 3:2-17
89. Luke 4:3-12
90. Luke 4:18-21
91. John 1:29-34
92. John 1:51
93. John 4:ff
94. John 5:ff
95. John 8: 311-51
96. John 9:1-39
97. Matthew 16:13-19
98. St. Matthew 10:7
99. St. Luke 10:17
100. Mark 10:35
101. Mark 10:41
102. Romans 13:14
103. Ephesians 4:15
104. Galatians 2:20
105. Colossians 1:15
106. Luke 17:20-21
107. This sequence from Mark 12:28-34
108. Paraphrase of John 14:10-11
109. John 10:30
110. These words are mine, the personal understanding of what I acknowledge Jesus to be saying in his witness to the kingdom of God.
111. Hebrews 9:11-12
112. John 1:29
113. Mark 14:61
114. John 19:5-7
115. Mark 14 55-59

116. John 11:50
117. Matthew 3:15
118. Wisdom of Solomon, chapter 2
119. Luke 22:42
120. Luke 23:34
121. John 19:30
122. Luke 23: 46
123. Mark 8:34-37
124. Acts 1:4
125. John 14:8-10
126. John 10:22-30
127. John 17:20-26
128. Luke 2:49
129. John 14:12-20
130. John 14:21
131. Acts 1:3-5
132. Acts 2:1-17
133. Acts 4:19-20
134. Matthew 27:45-47
135. John 19:30
136. Luke 24:6
137. Colossians 1:27-28 and 2:8-15
138. Romans 11:32
139. 1 Corinthians 15:22
140. 1 Corinthians 15:28
141. John 4:21-24
142. John 1:18 and 6:46
143. 1 John 4:9-11
144. John 13:34-35
145. John 13:15
146. 1 Corinthians 11:25
147. 1 Corinthians 11:26
148. John 17:25-26
149. 1 John 4:8
150. 1 Corinthians 8:5-6
151. John 6:33
152. Romans 13:8-10
153. Matthew 5:46-48
154. Taken from 1 Corinthians 12:4-14:1
155. John 3:16
156. The Book of Common Prayer, p. 427
157. See Matthew 16:24ff and 10:38ff; Luke 14:27ff and 17:33; and Mark 8:34ff

158. Acts 9:2
159. Acts 2:43-47 and 4:32-35
160. Matthew 5:39-42
161. 1 Corinthians 12:24-26
162. 1 Corinthians 11:23-25
163. John 14:18
164. Colossians 1:27
165. Acts 2:42-47
166. 1 Corinthians 11:26
167. John 13:15-17
168. Matthew 18:20
169. A collage of Jesus' words from the Gospels. I trust you to know them already.
170. Scriptures from this paragraph: Genesis 1: 27 and 22:17; Matthew 26:28; John 12:32; 1 Corinthians 12:13; Ephesians 2:14
171. Building on Ephesians 4:4
172. John 6:28-29
173. Matthew 7:1-5
174. John 21:21-22
175. Luke 17:10
176. From Luke 8:48-50 and John 8:36, 51; 14:20
177. Matthew 28:18-20
178. From Matthew 7:28
179. Acts 8:18-23
180. Mark 7:20-23
181. Romans 1:20-24
182. John 8:32-33
183. Matthew 10:25 and Luke 6:40
184. From Matthew 28:19-20 with my paraphrase
185. From Luke 6:40; Matthew 10:25; John 13:20, 10:30, and 17:22
186. Acts 2:40
187. Philippians 2:12-13
188. 2 Corinthians 5:14-21
189. Ephesians 1:23
190. Romans 5:8-10
191. John 1:27 and 34
192. John 1:39
193. Matthew 18:21-22
194. Might this somehow be the intent of Jesus' statement in Mark 3:28-30?
195. Ephesians 4:13